Ismyre

A FANTASY MYSTERY
STORY

BY B. MURE

AVERY HILL PUBLISHING
LONDON

Published by Avery Hill Publishing, 2017

10 9 8 7 6 5 4 3 2 1

First published in the UK in 2017 by
Avery Hill Publishing
Office 7
35 Ludgate Hill
London
EC4M 7JN

A CIP record for this book is available from the British Library

ISBN: 978 1 910395 34 9

B. Mure
www.bmurecreative.co.uk

Avery Hill Publishing
www.averyhillpublishing.com

THE SCULPTOR CARVES
BECAUSE HE MUST

BARBARA HEPWORTH

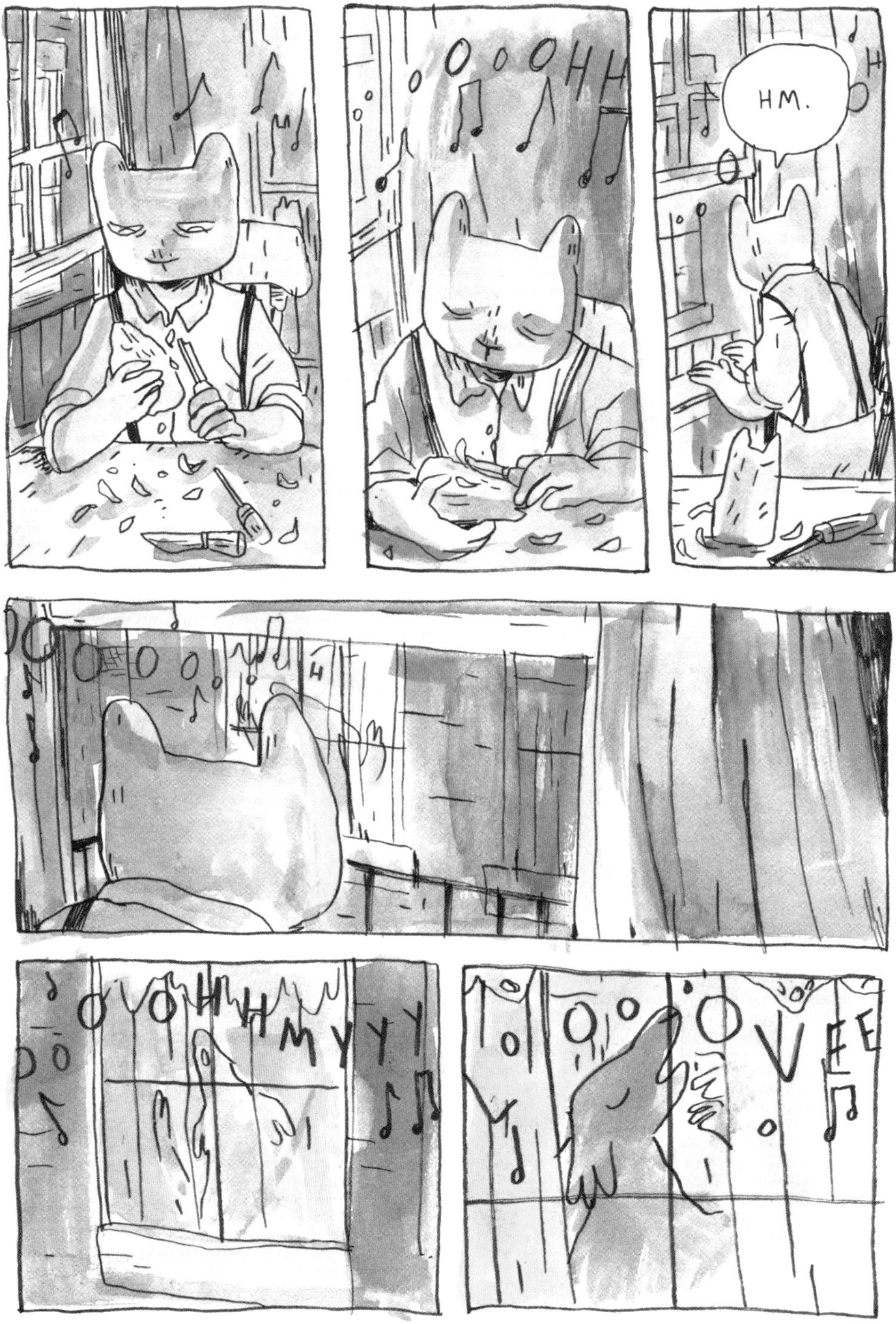
OOOHH
HM.
OOOHHMYYY
OOOVE

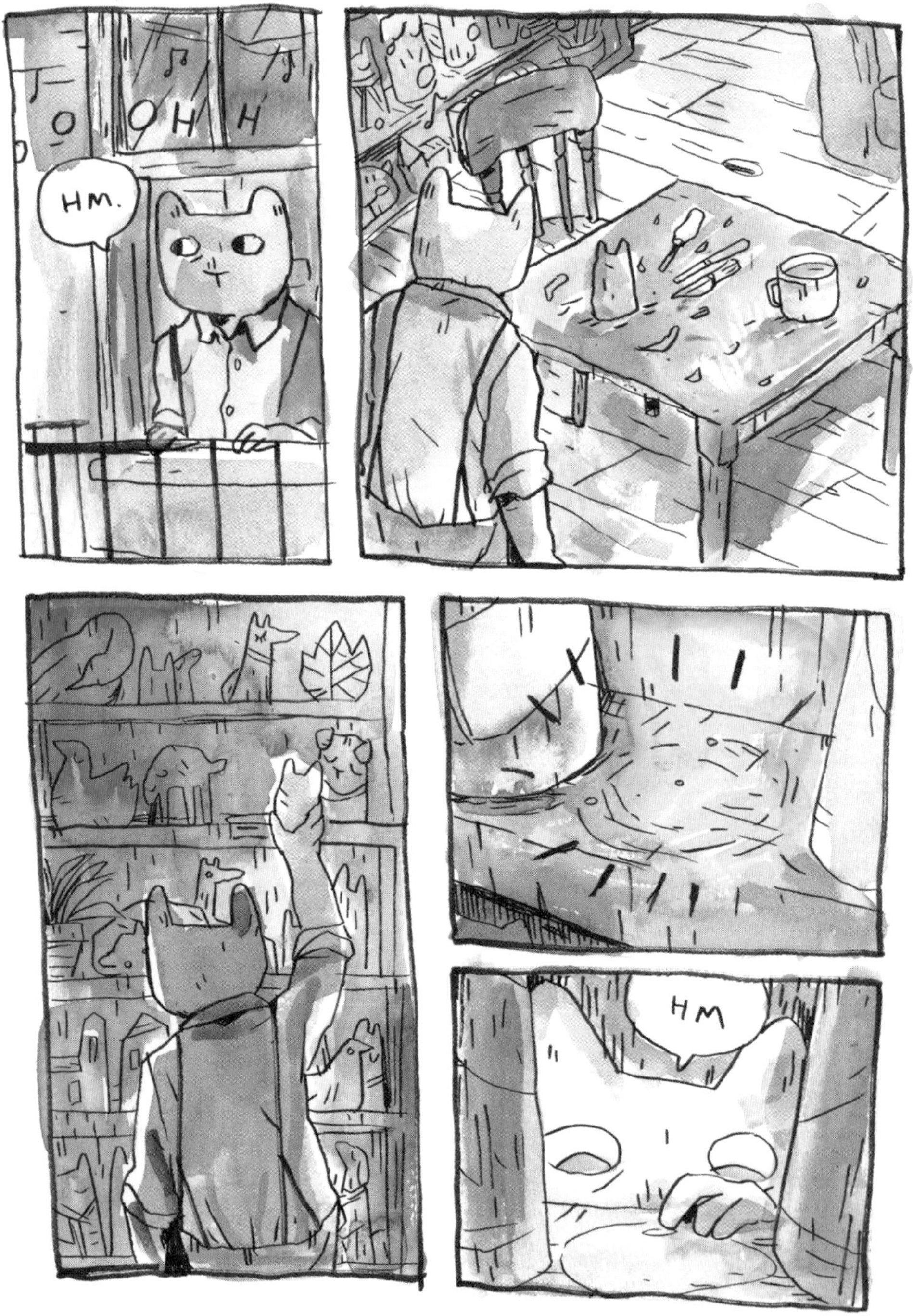
OOHH
HM.
HM

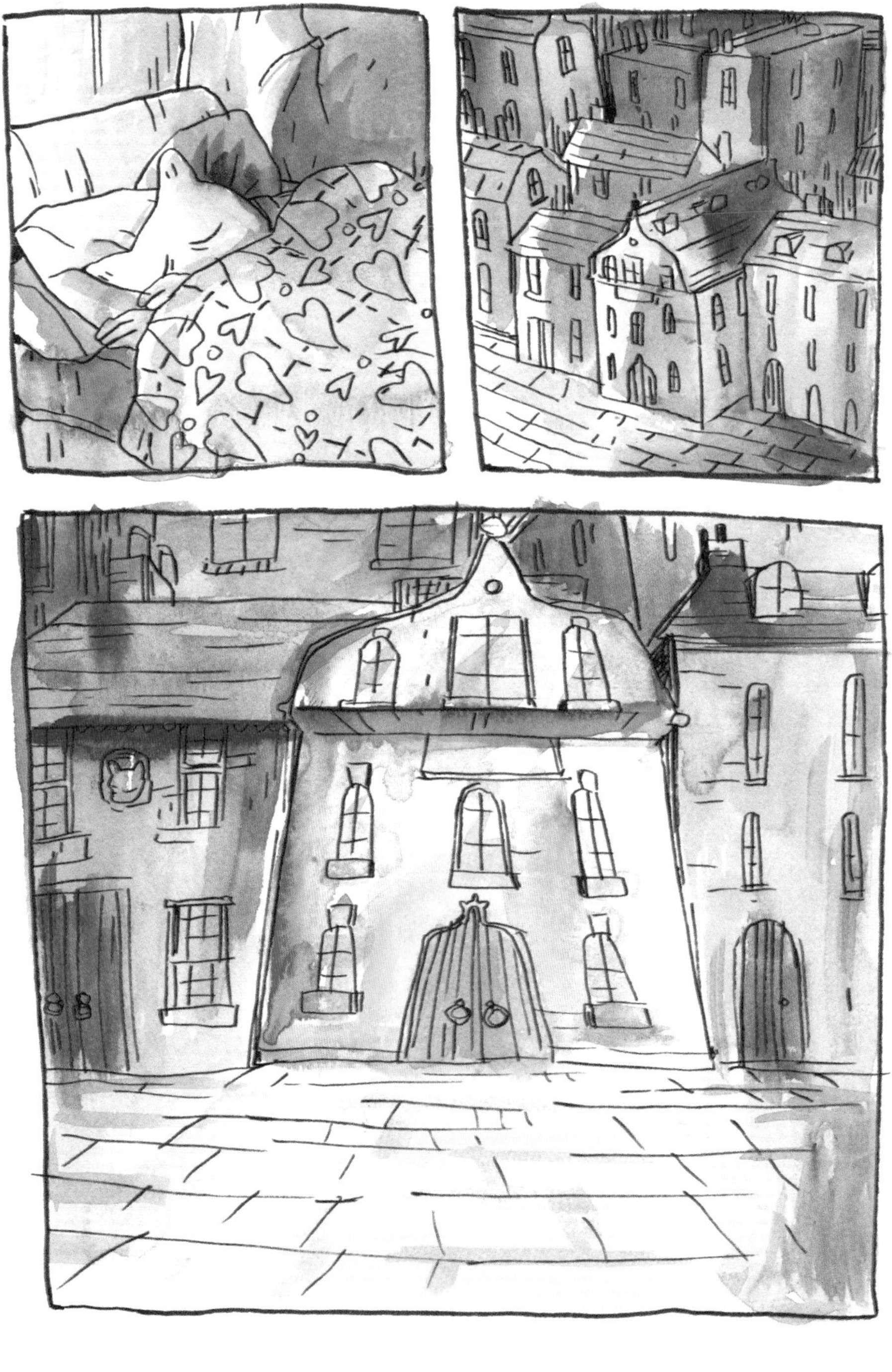

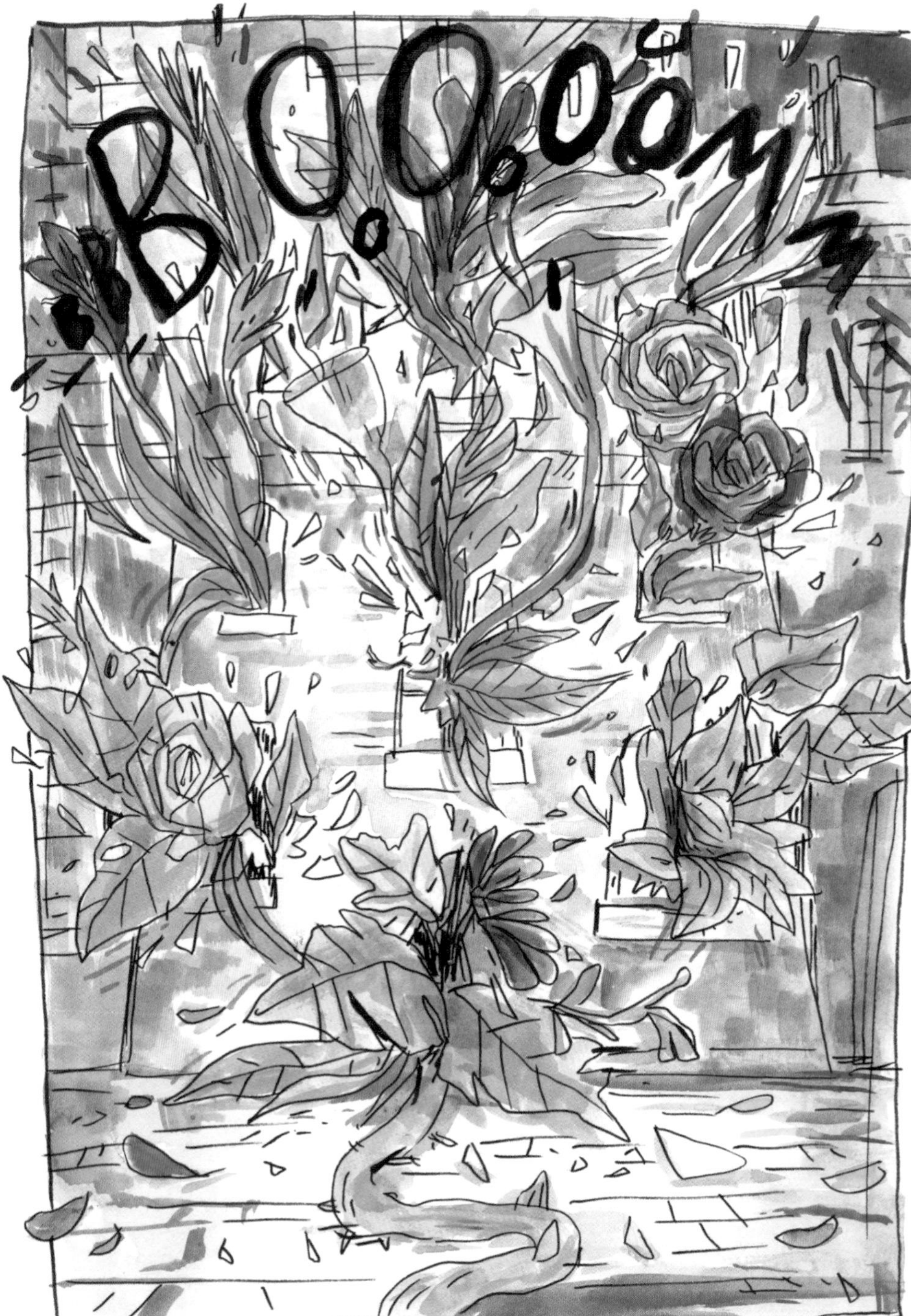
BOOOOOOOM

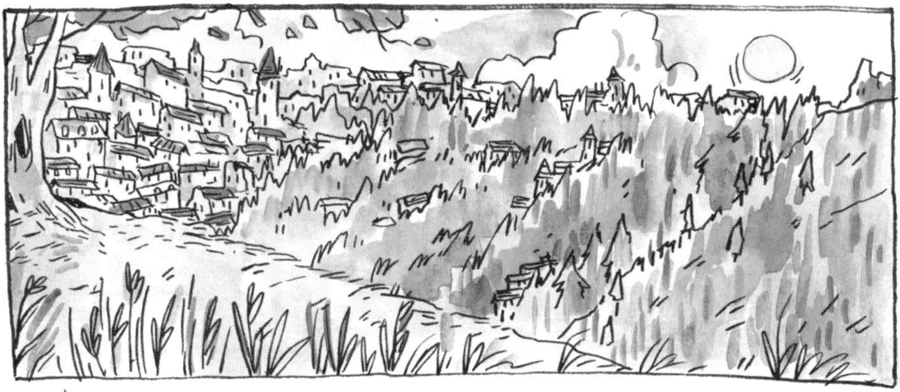

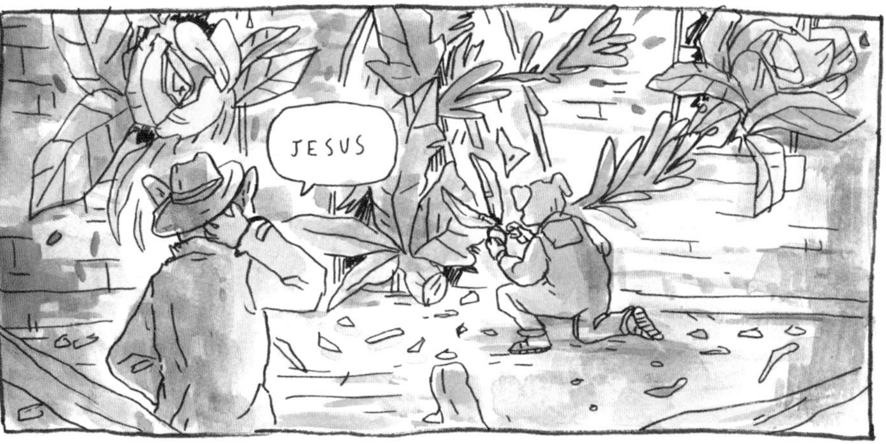
JESUS

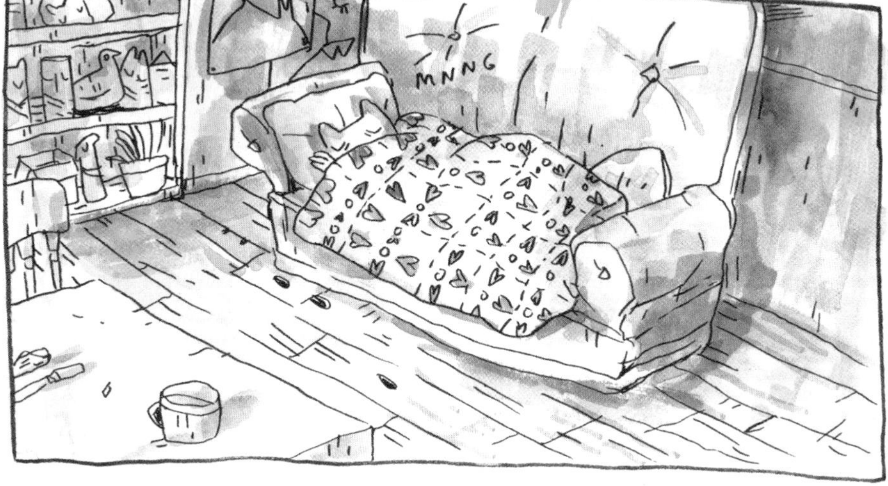
MNNG

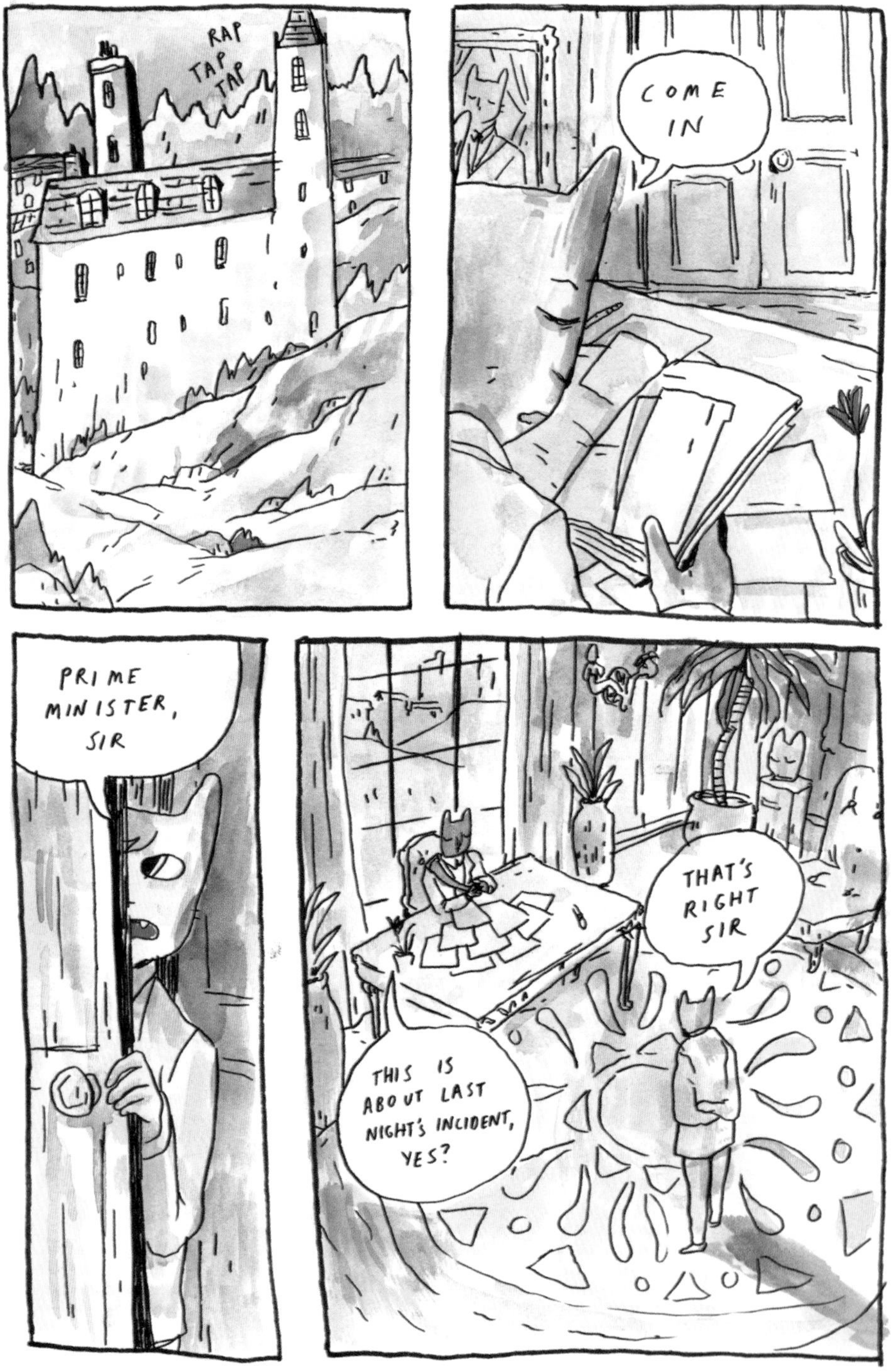
RAP TAP TAP
COME IN
PRIME MINISTER, SIR
THIS IS ABOUT LAST NIGHT'S INCIDENT, YES?
THAT'S RIGHT SIR

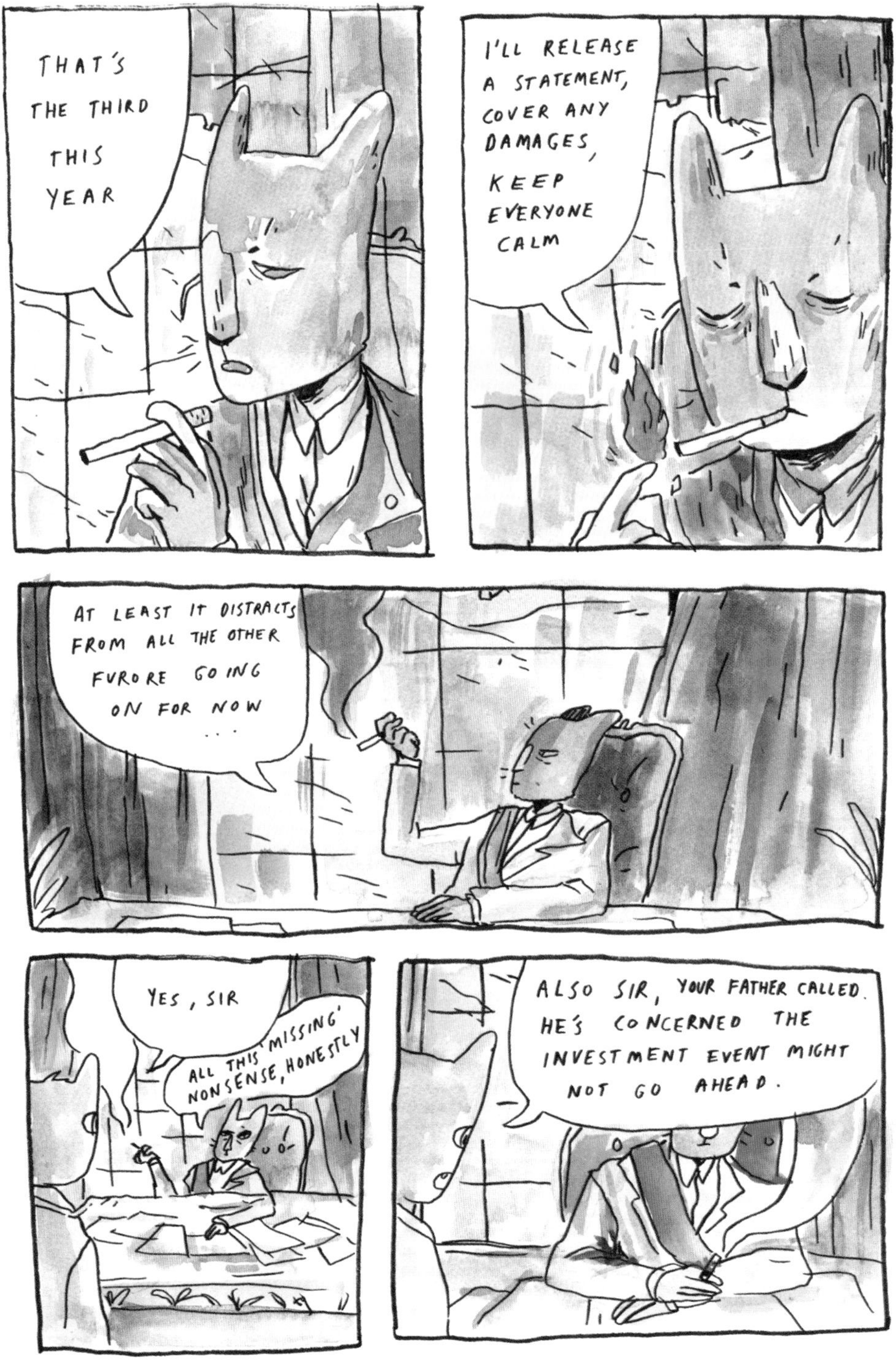
THAT'S THE THIRD THIS YEAR
I'LL RELEASE A STATEMENT, COVER ANY DAMAGES, KEEP EVERYONE CALM
AT LEAST IT DISTRACTS FROM ALL THE OTHER FURORE GOING ON FOR NOW ...
YES, SIR
ALL THIS 'MISSING' NONSENSE, HONESTLY
ALSO SIR, YOUR FATHER CALLED. HE'S CONCERNED THE INVESTMENT EVENT MIGHT NOT GO AHEAD.

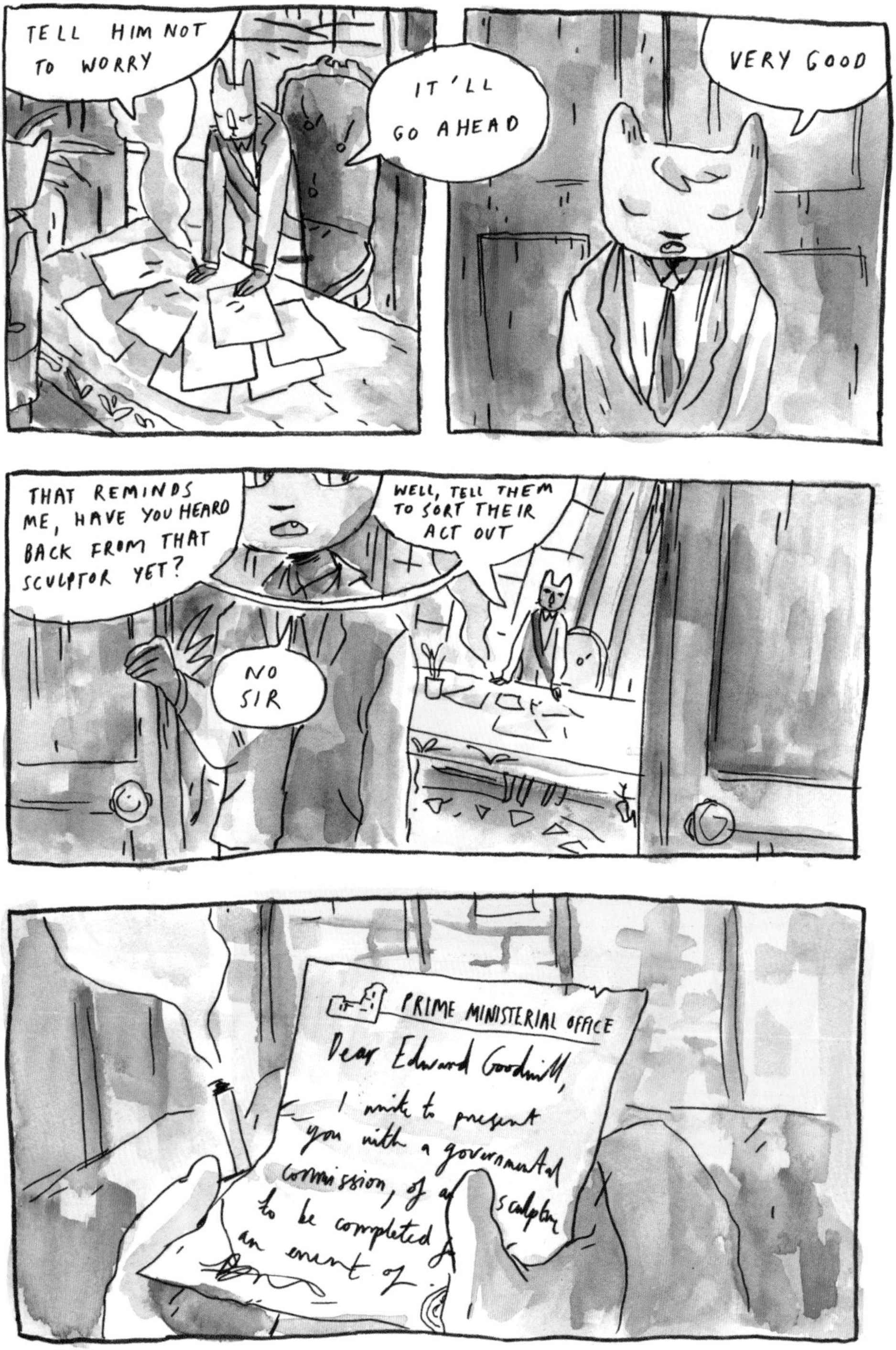
TELL HIM NOT TO WORRY
IT'LL GO AHEAD
VERY GOOD
THAT REMINDS ME, HAVE YOU HEARD BACK FROM THAT SCULPTOR YET?
NO SIR
WELL, TELL THEM TO SORT THEIR ACT OUT
PRIME MINISTERIAL OFFICE
Dear Edward Goodwill,
I write to present
you with a governmental
commission, of a
sculpture
to be completed
an event of

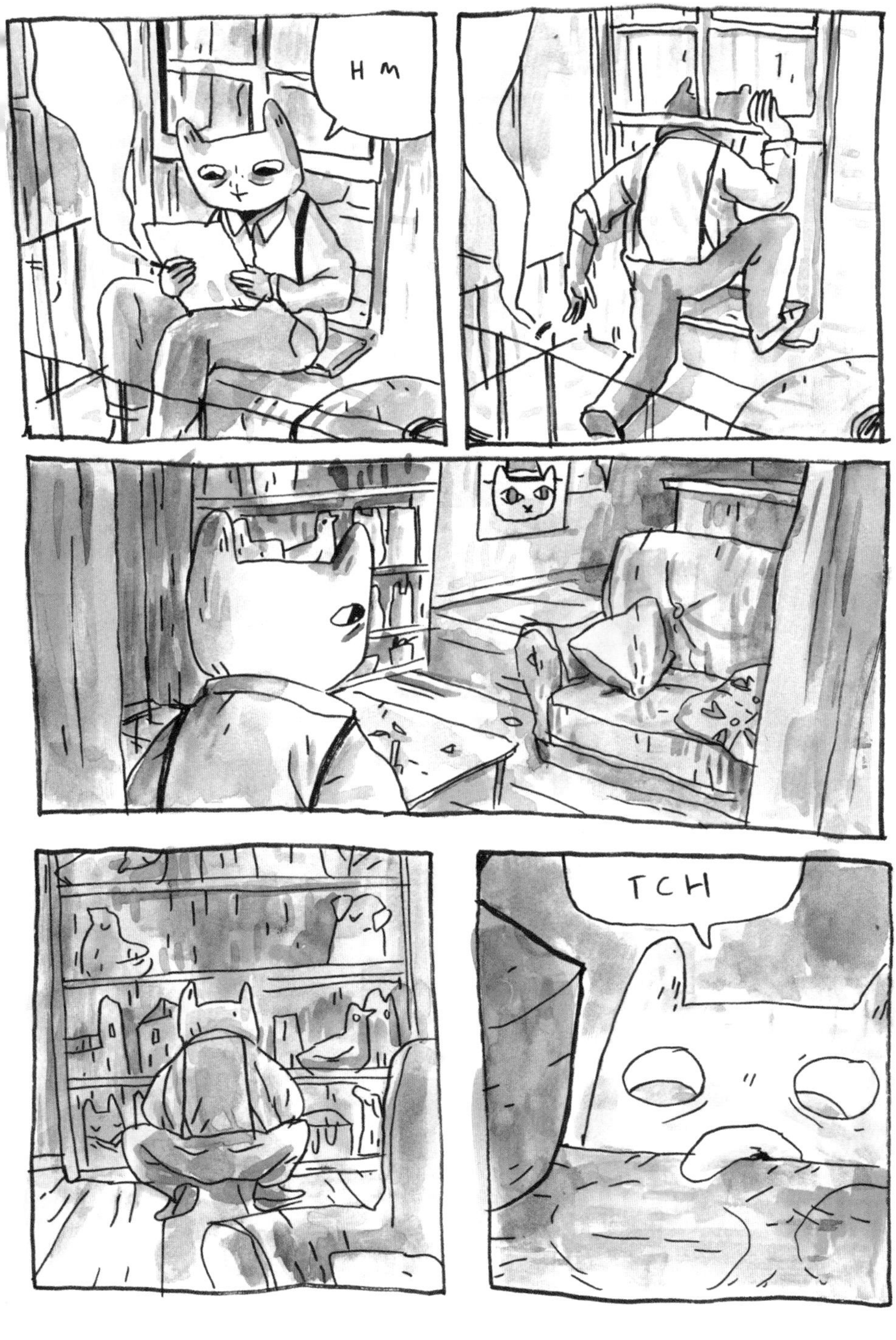
H M
TCH

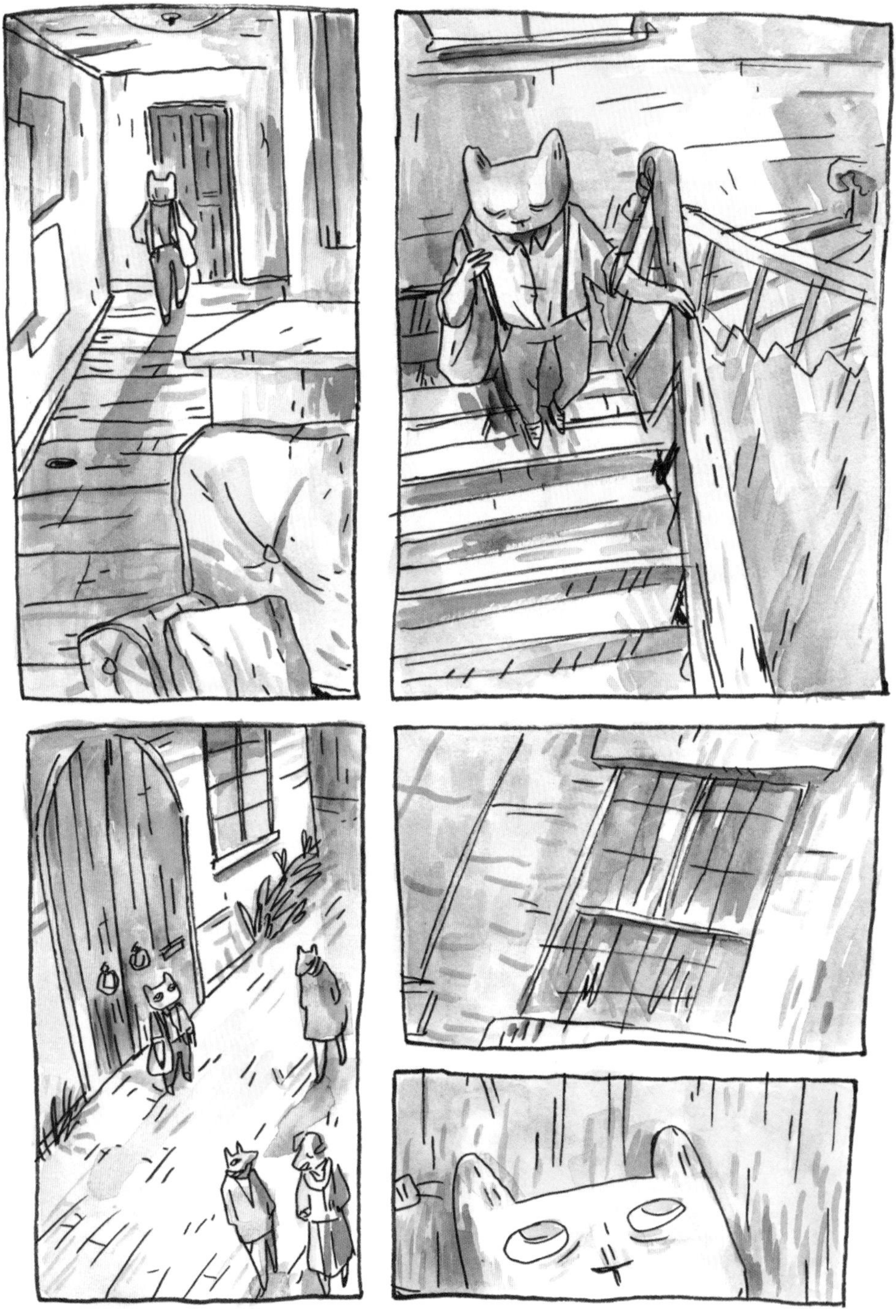

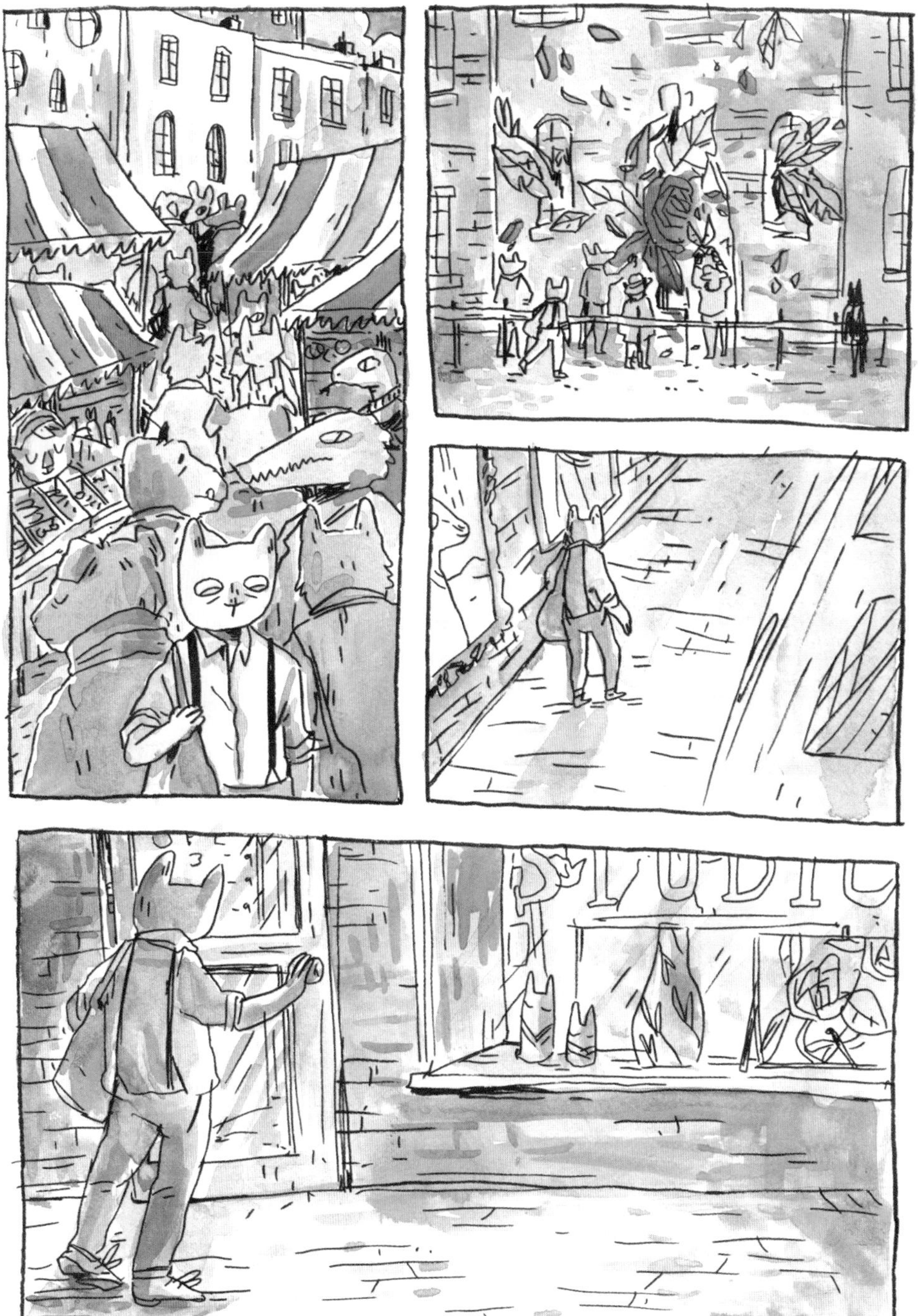

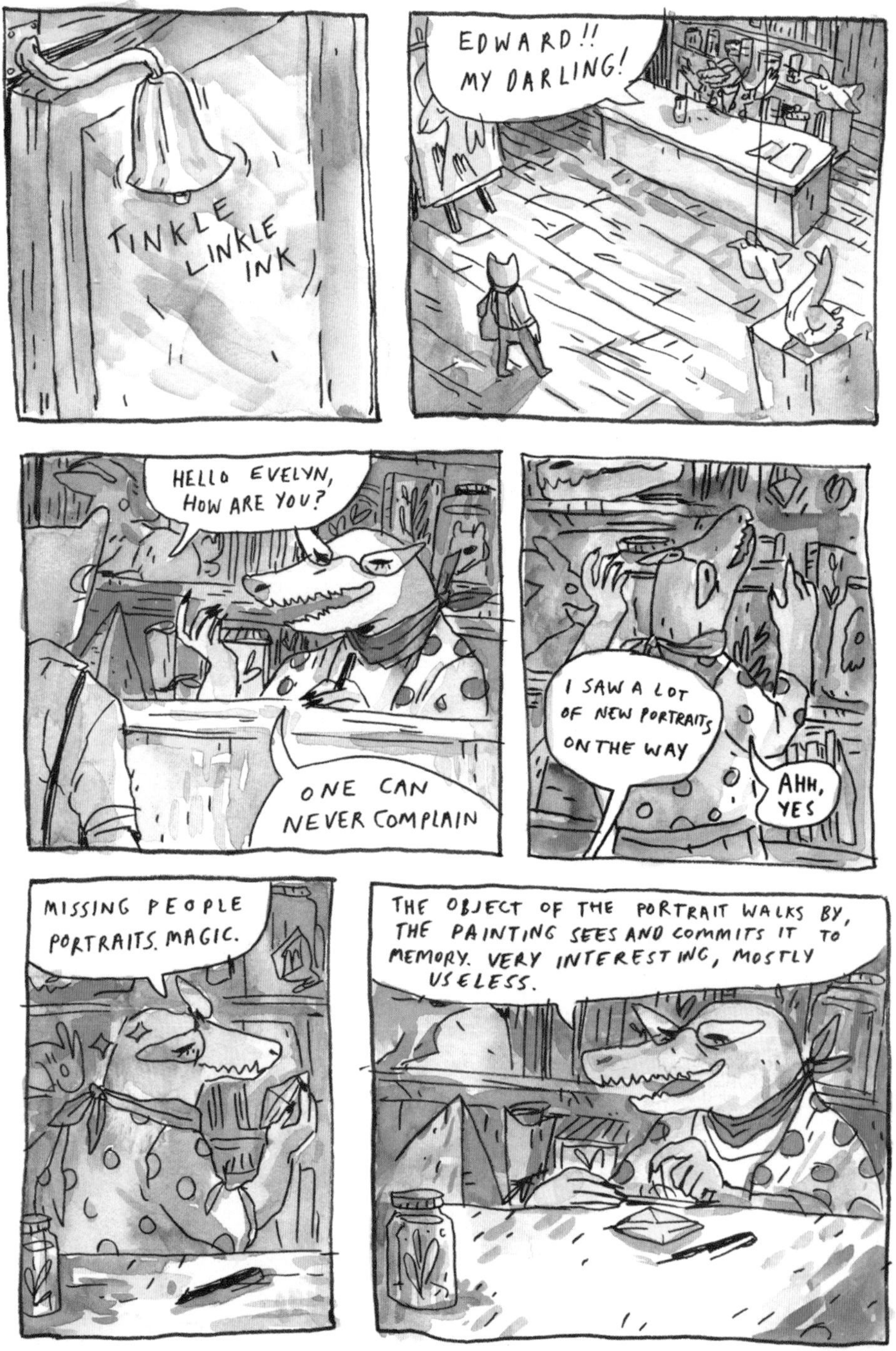
TINKLE LINKLE INK
EDWARD!! MY DARLING!
HELLO EVELYN, HOW ARE YOU?
ONE CAN NEVER COMPLAIN
I SAW A LOT OF NEW PORTRAITS ON THE WAY
AHH, YES
MISSING PEOPLE PORTRAITS. MAGIC.
THE OBJECT OF THE PORTRAIT WALKS BY, THE PAINTING SEES AND COMMITS IT TO MEMORY. VERY INTERESTING, MOSTLY USELESS.

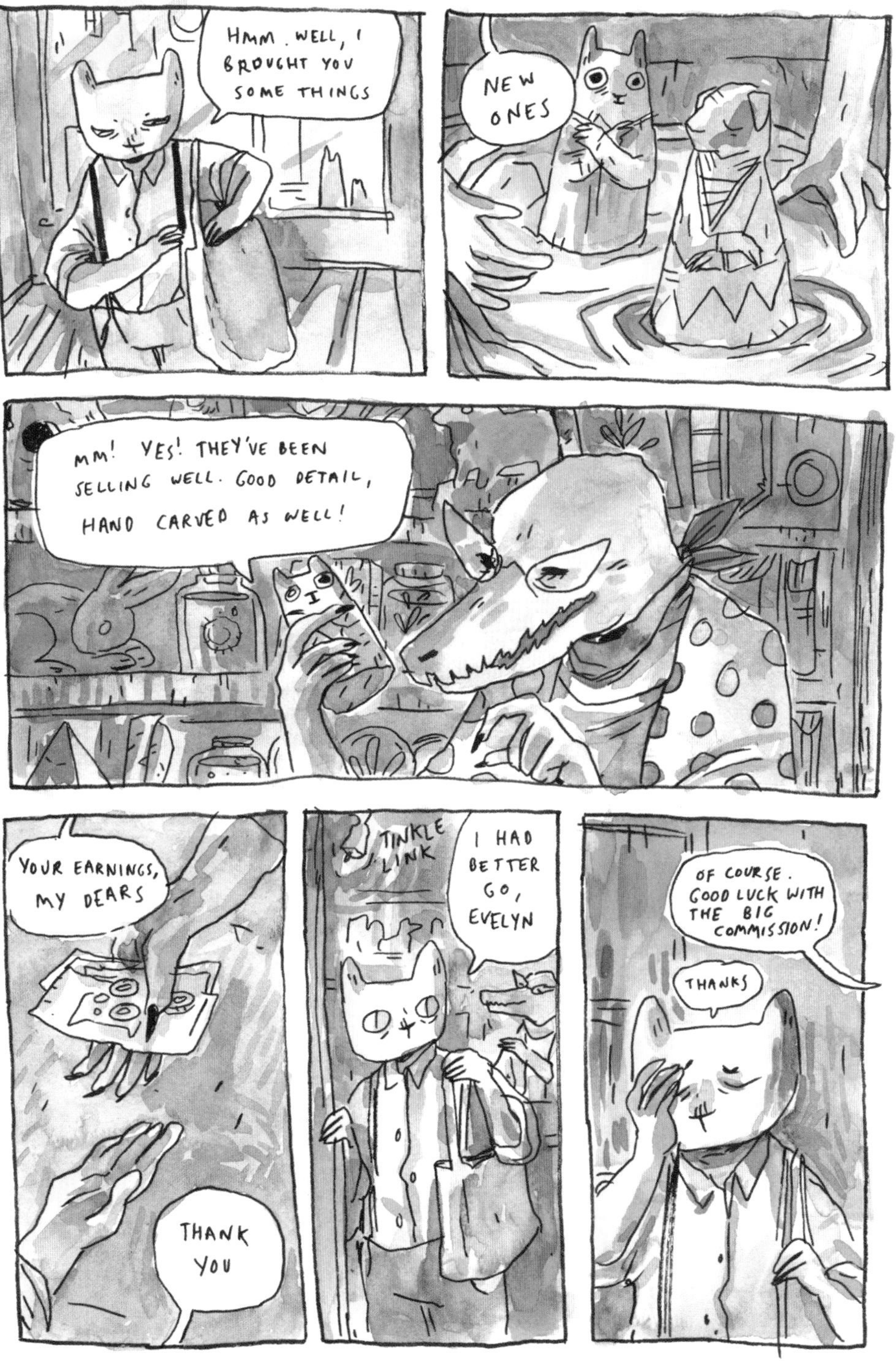
HMM. WELL, I BROUGHT YOU SOME THINGS
NEW ONES
MM! YES! THEY'VE BEEN SELLING WELL. GOOD DETAIL, HAND CARVED AS WELL!
YOUR EARNINGS, MY DEARS
THANK YOU
TINKLE LINK
I HAD BETTER GO, EVELYN
OF COURSE. GOOD LUCK WITH THE BIG COMMISSION!
THANKS

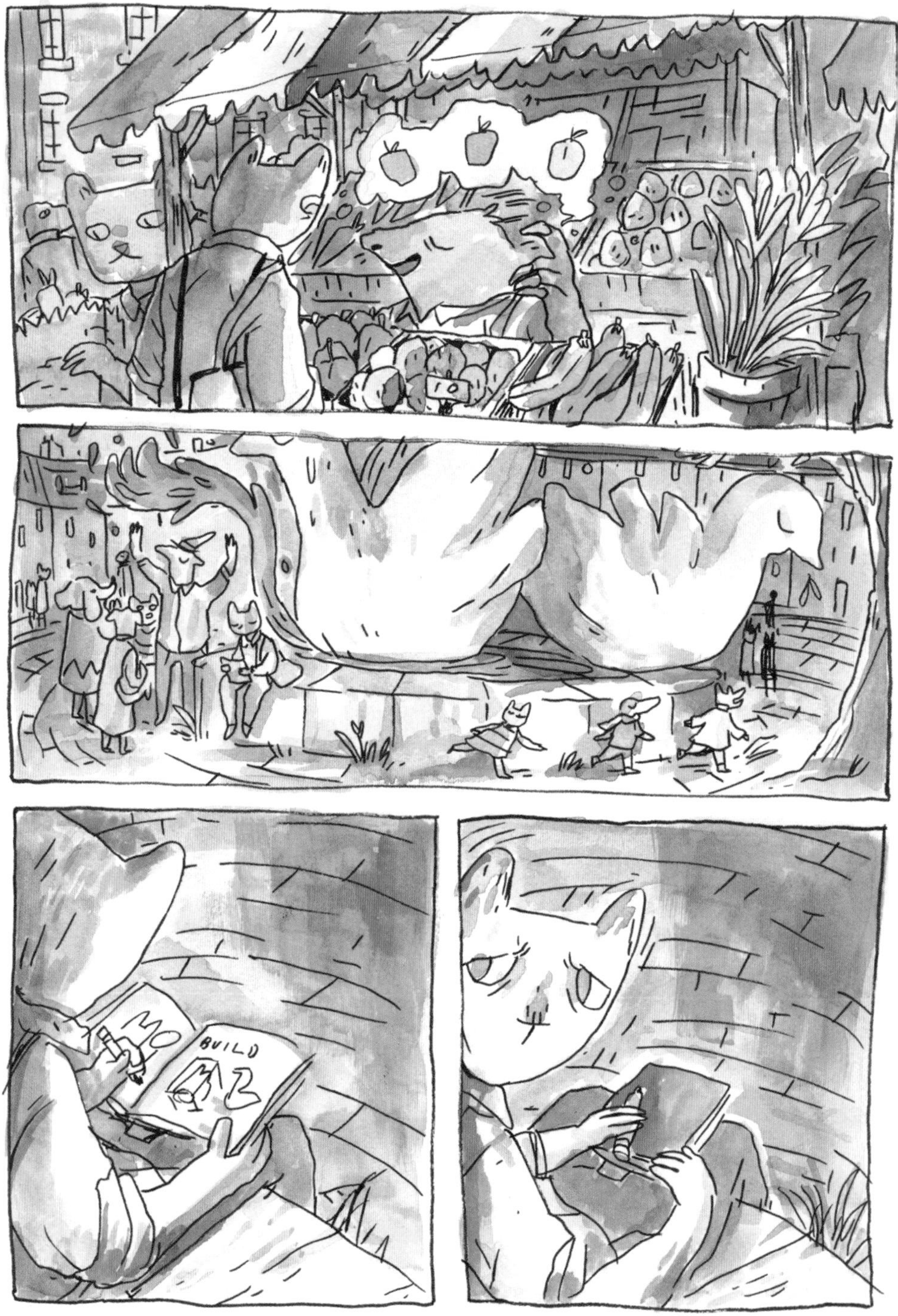
10
BUILD

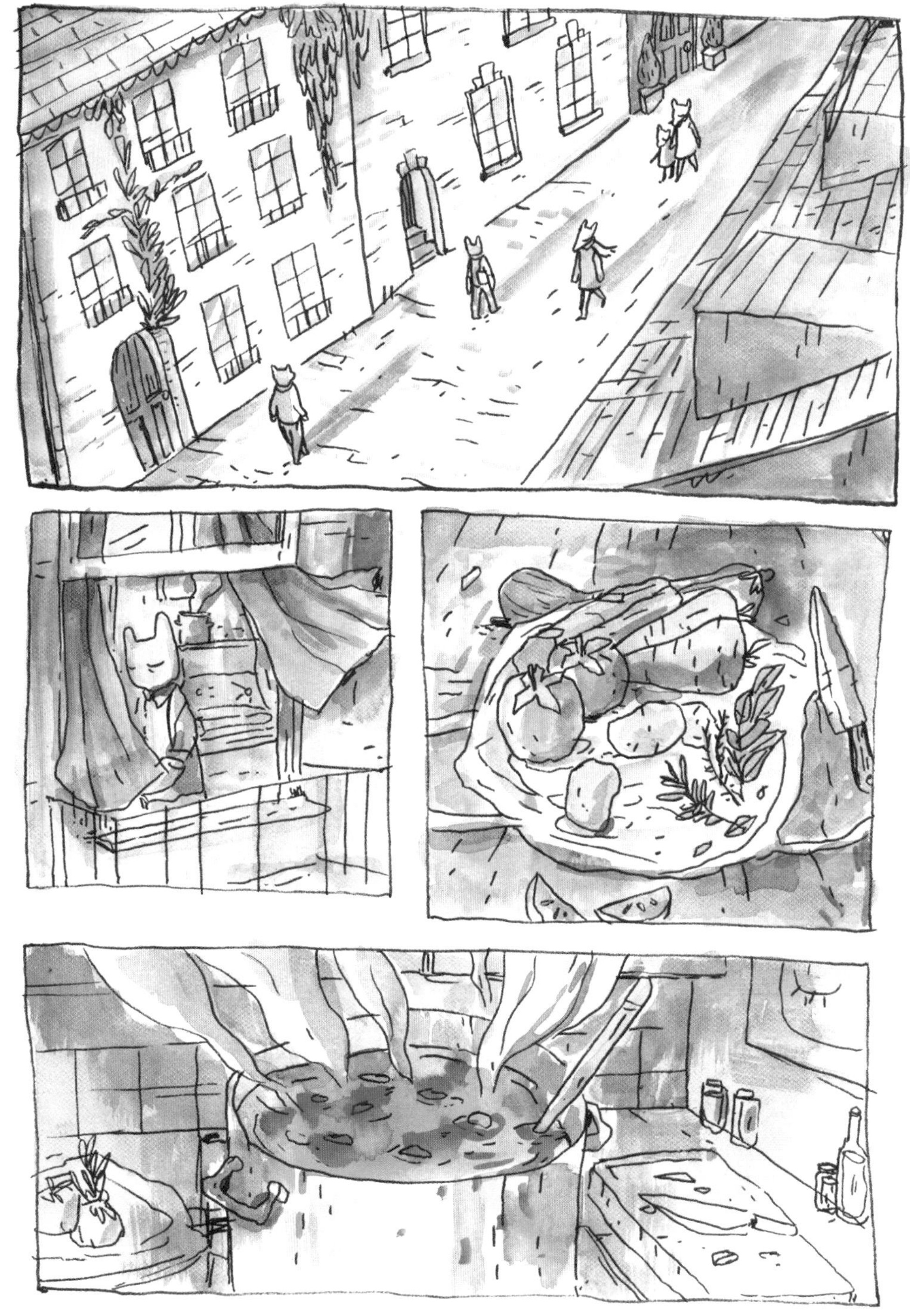

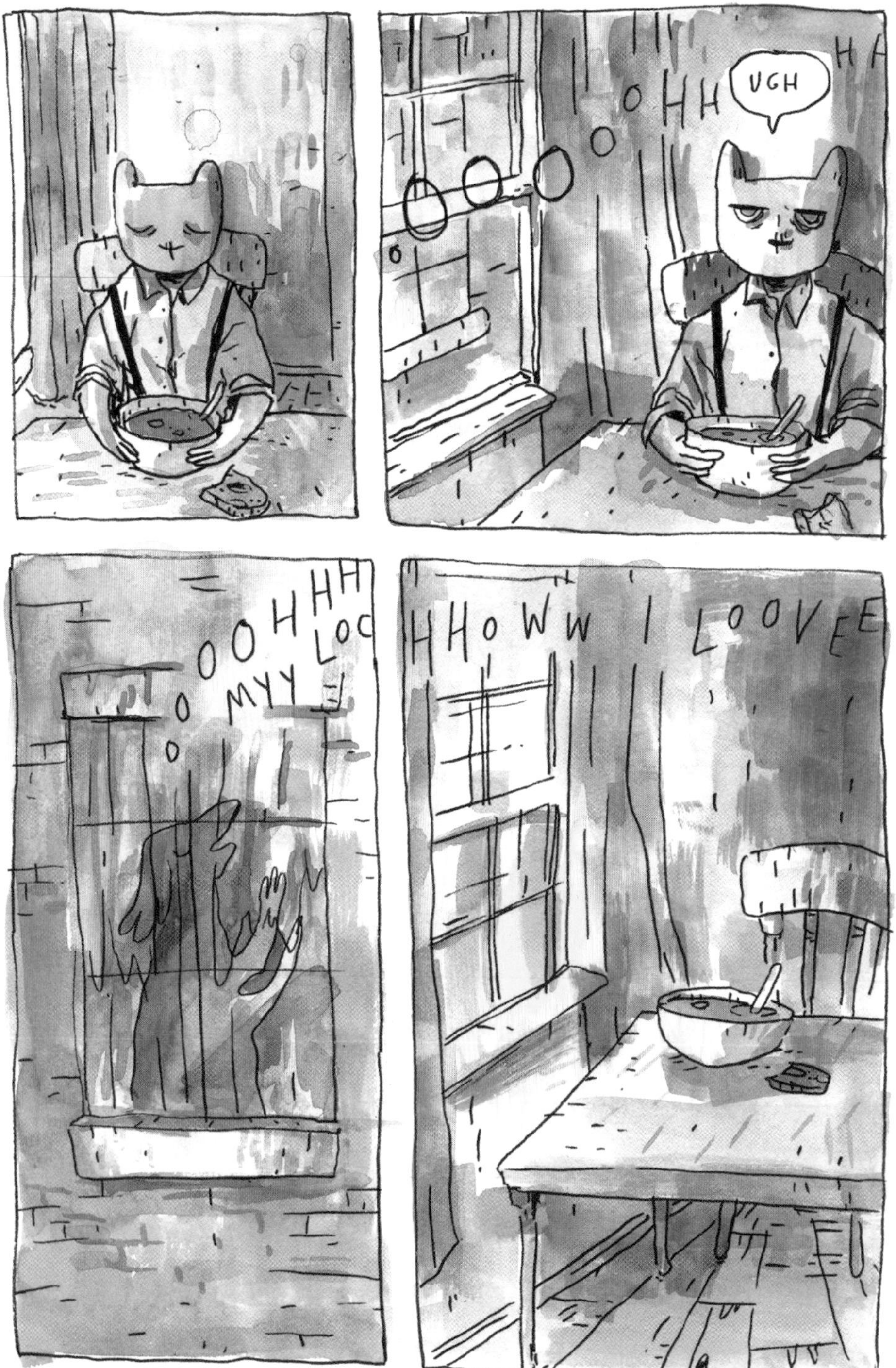
OHH
UGH
HA
OOHHHH
O MYY
LOC
HHOWW I LOOVEE

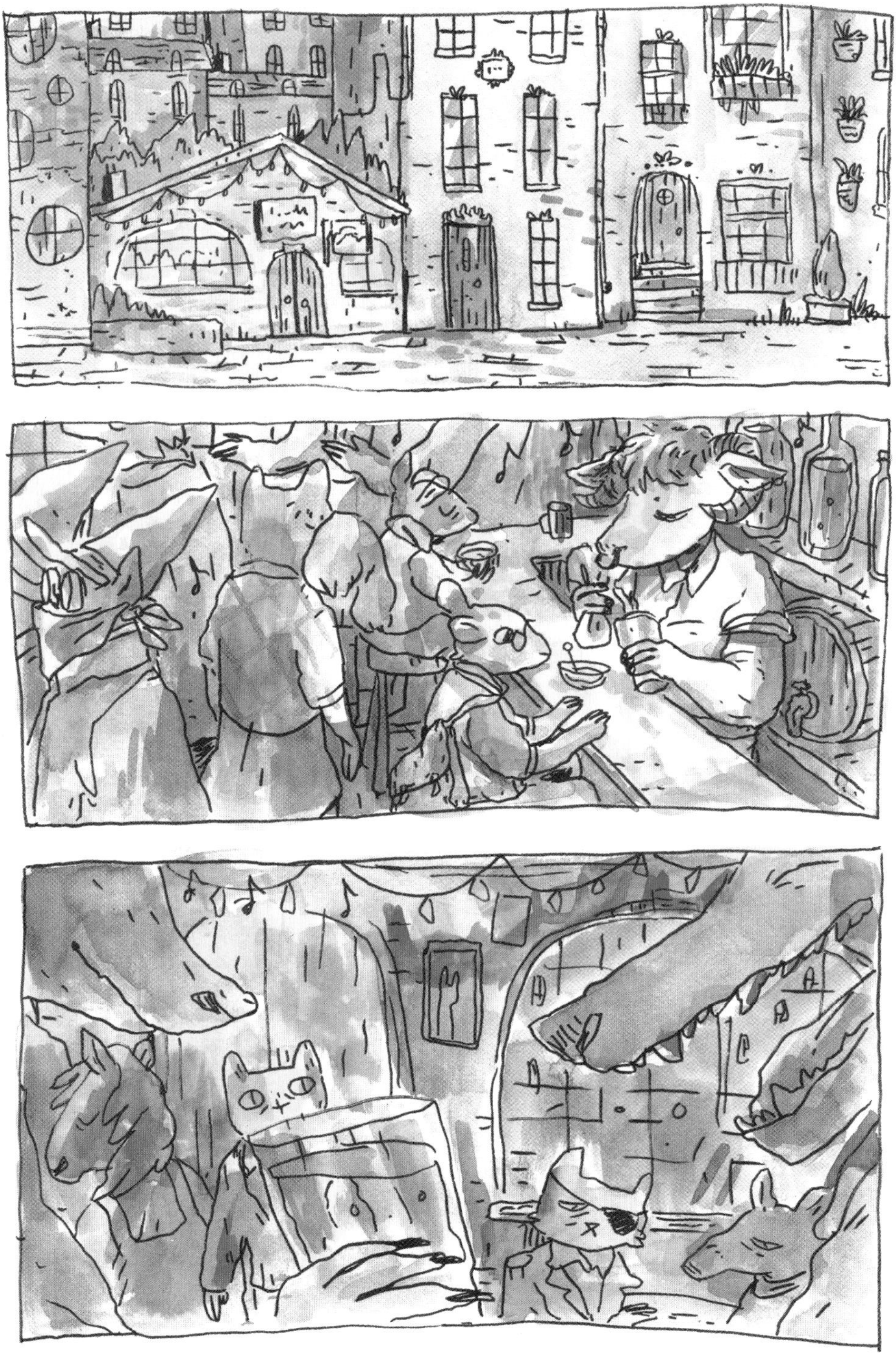

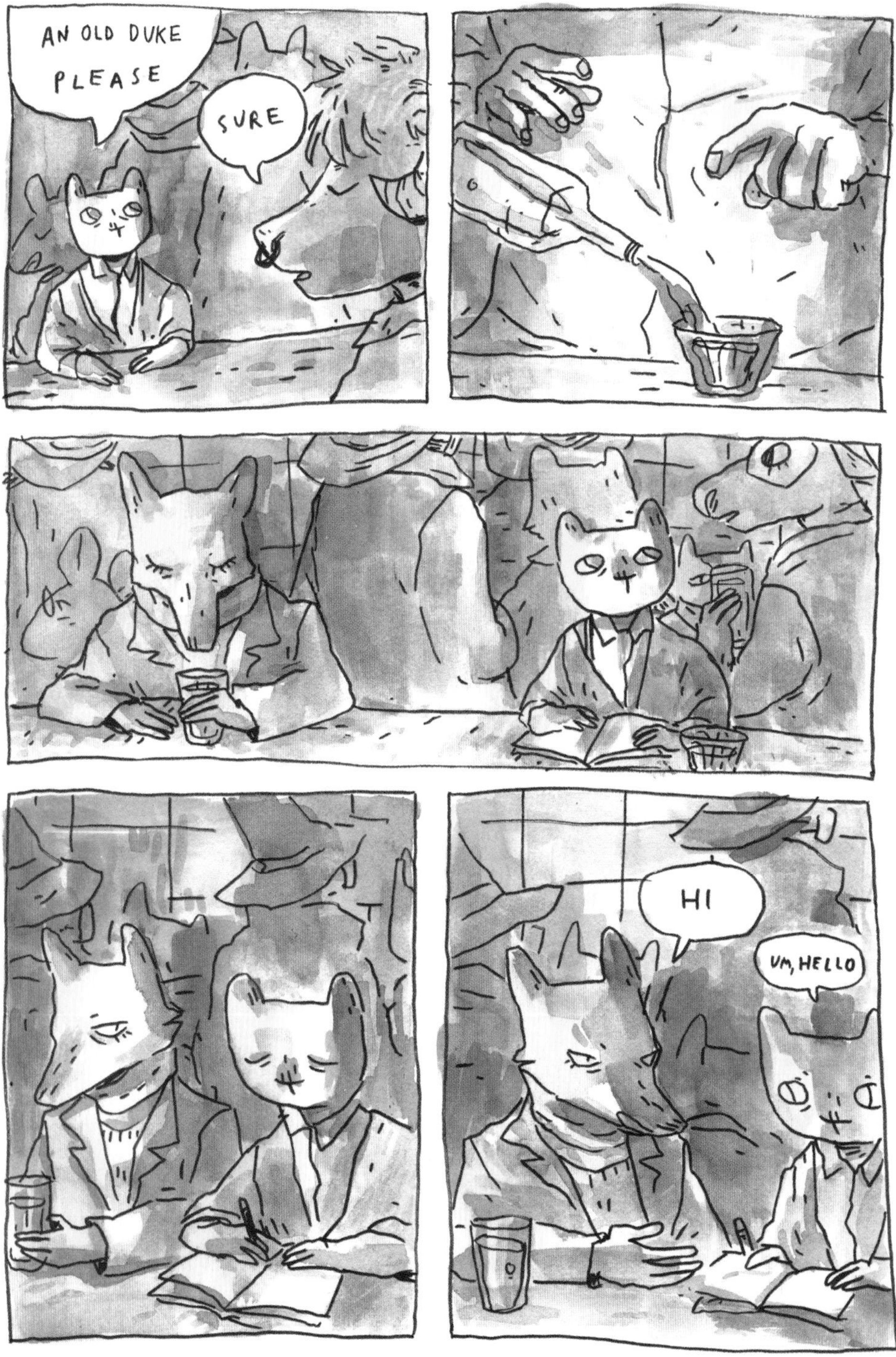
AN OLD DUKE PLEASE
SURE
HI
UM, HELLO

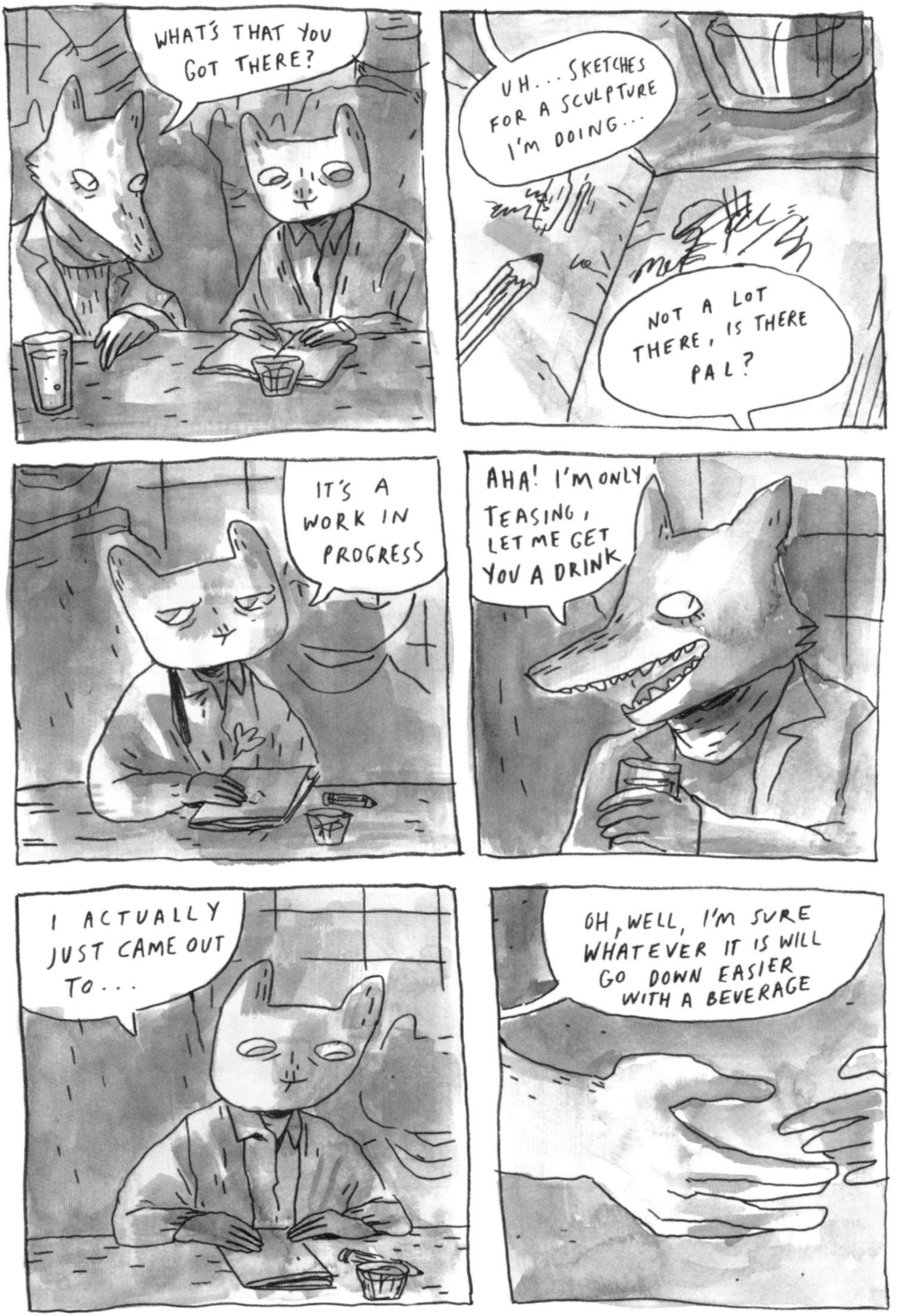
WHAT'S THAT YOU GOT THERE?
UH... SKETCHES FOR A SCULPTURE I'M DOING...
NOT A LOT THERE, IS THERE PAL?
IT'S A WORK IN PROGRESS
AHA! I'M ONLY TEASING, LET ME GET YOU A DRINK
I ACTUALLY JUST CAME OUT TO...
OH, WELL, I'M SURE WHATEVER IT IS WILL GO DOWN EASIER WITH A BEVERAGE

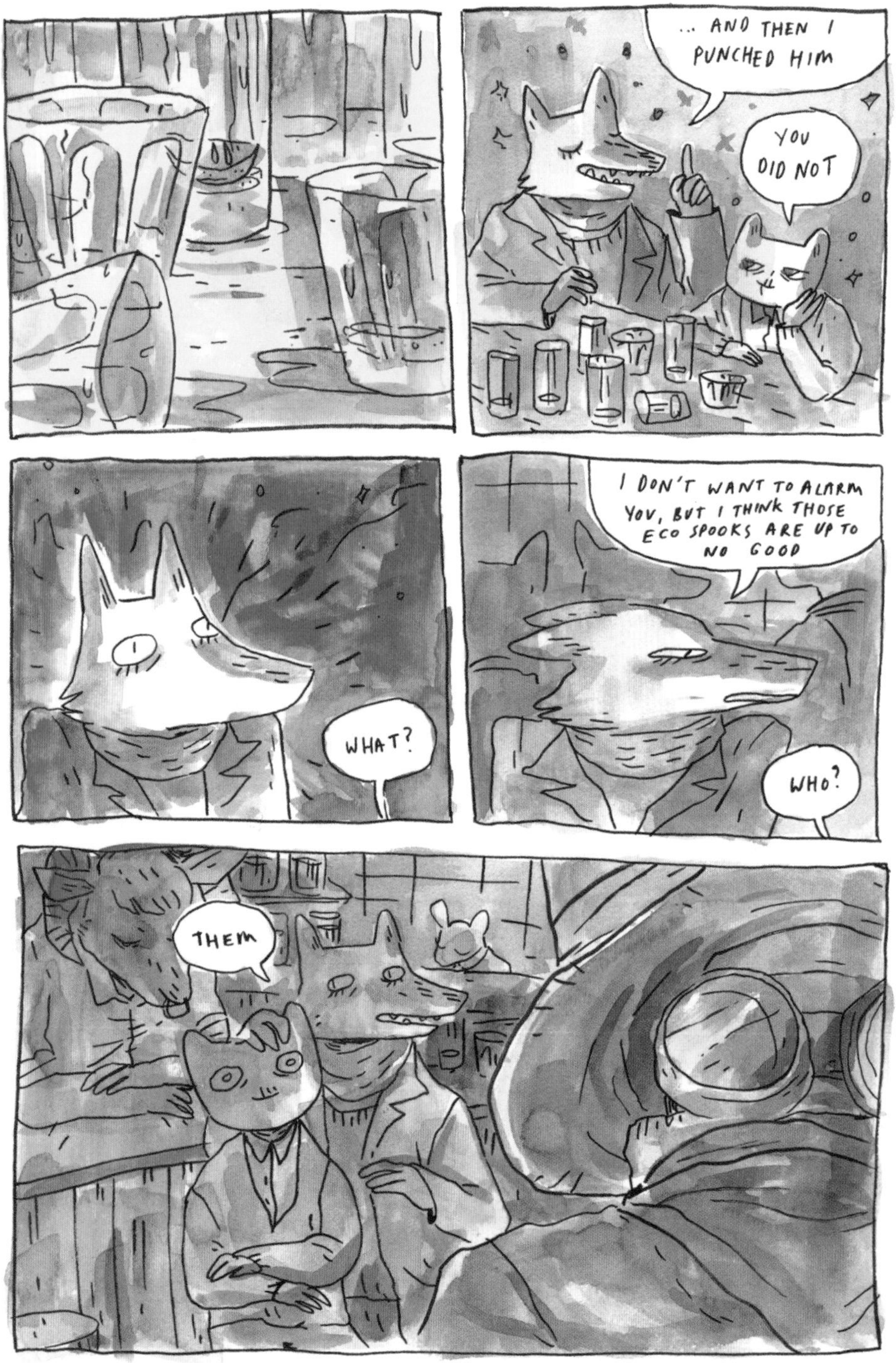
... AND THEN I PUNCHED HIM
YOU DID NOT
WHAT?
I DON'T WANT TO ALARM YOU, BUT I THINK THOSE ECO SPOOKS ARE UP TO NO GOOD
WHO?
THEM

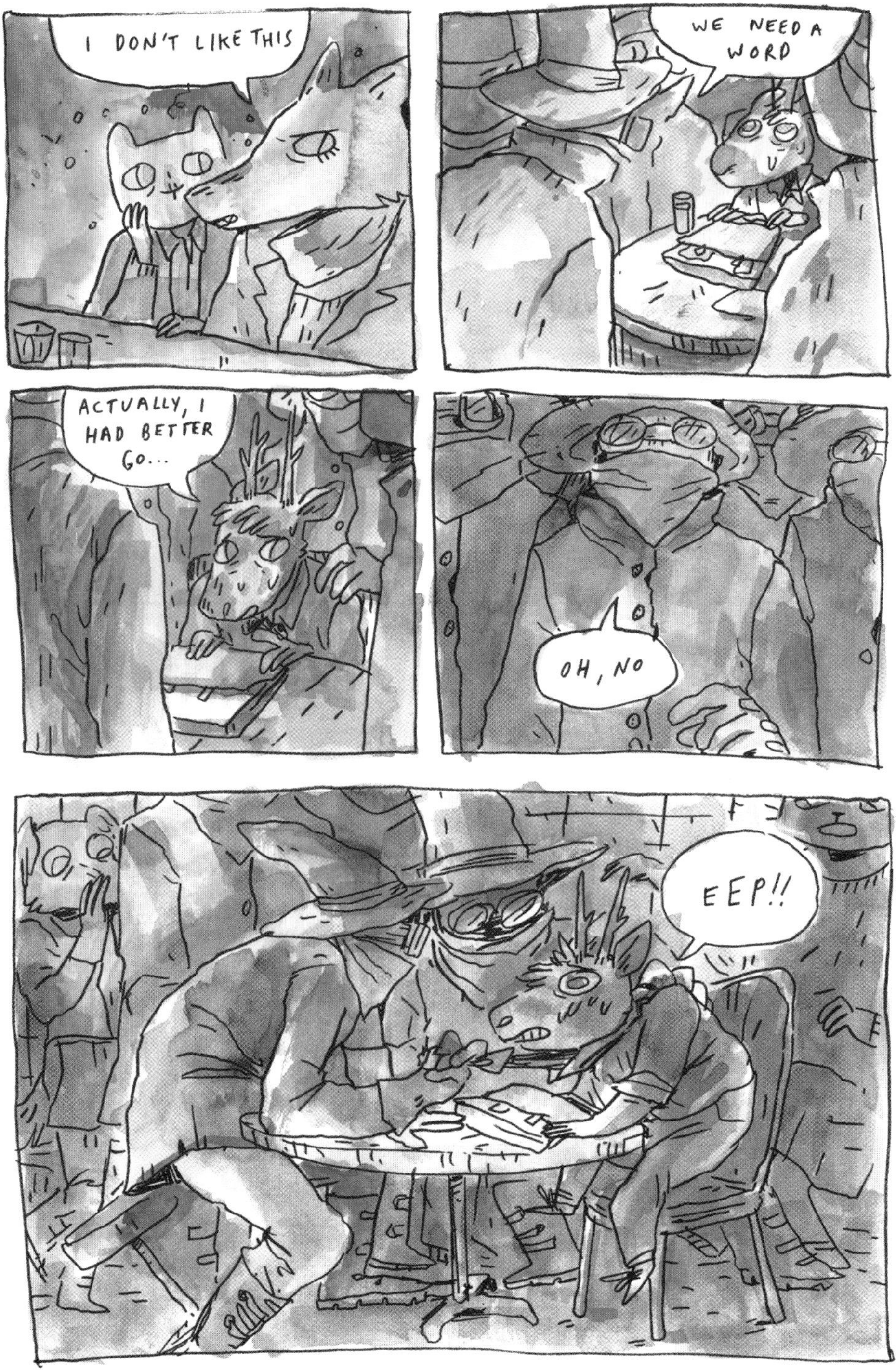
I DON'T LIKE THIS
WE NEED A WORD
ACTUALLY, I HAD BETTER GO...
OH, NO
EEP!!

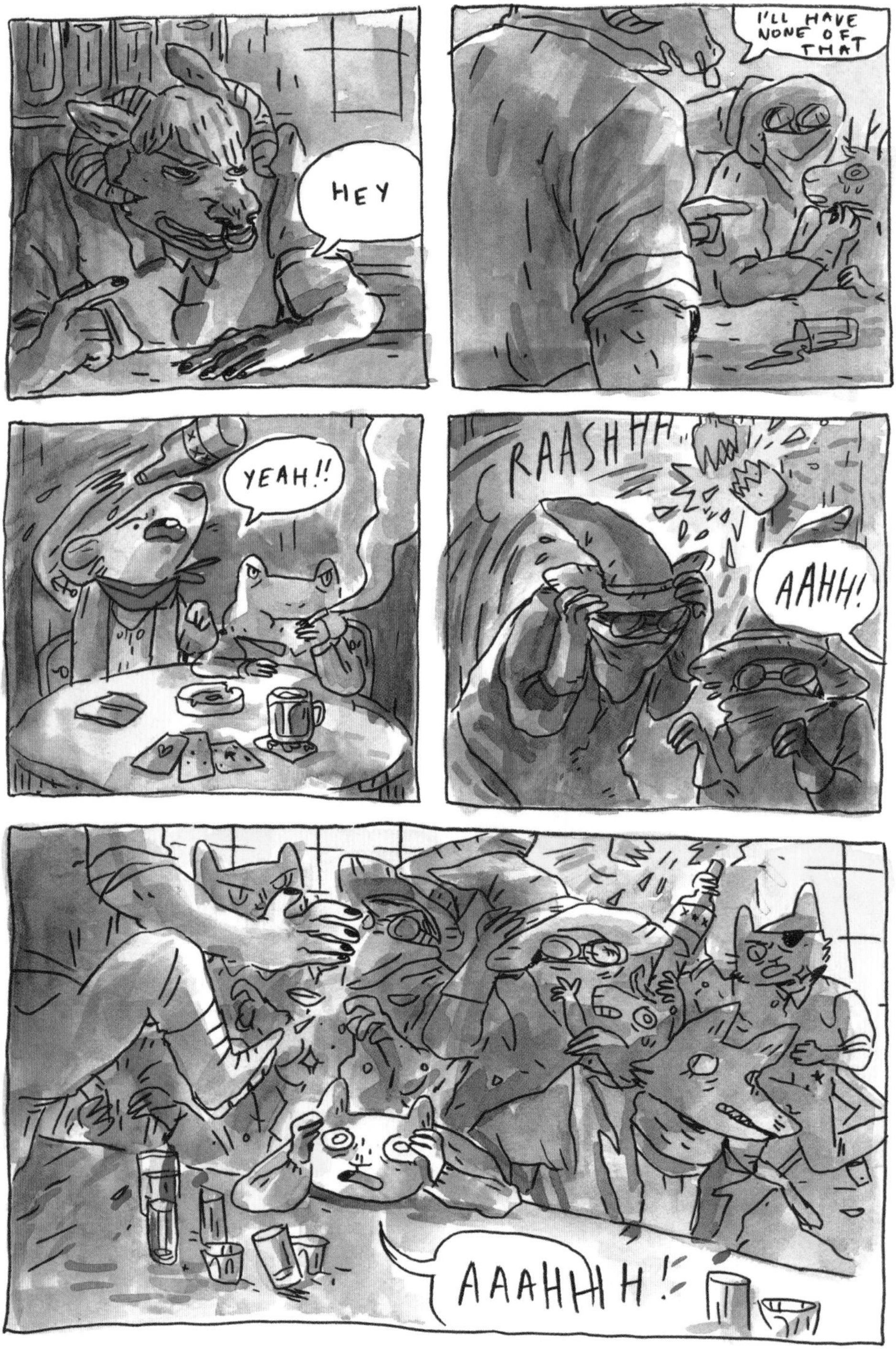
HEY
I'LL HAVE NONE OF THAT
YEAH!!
RAASHHH
AAHH!
AAAHHHH!

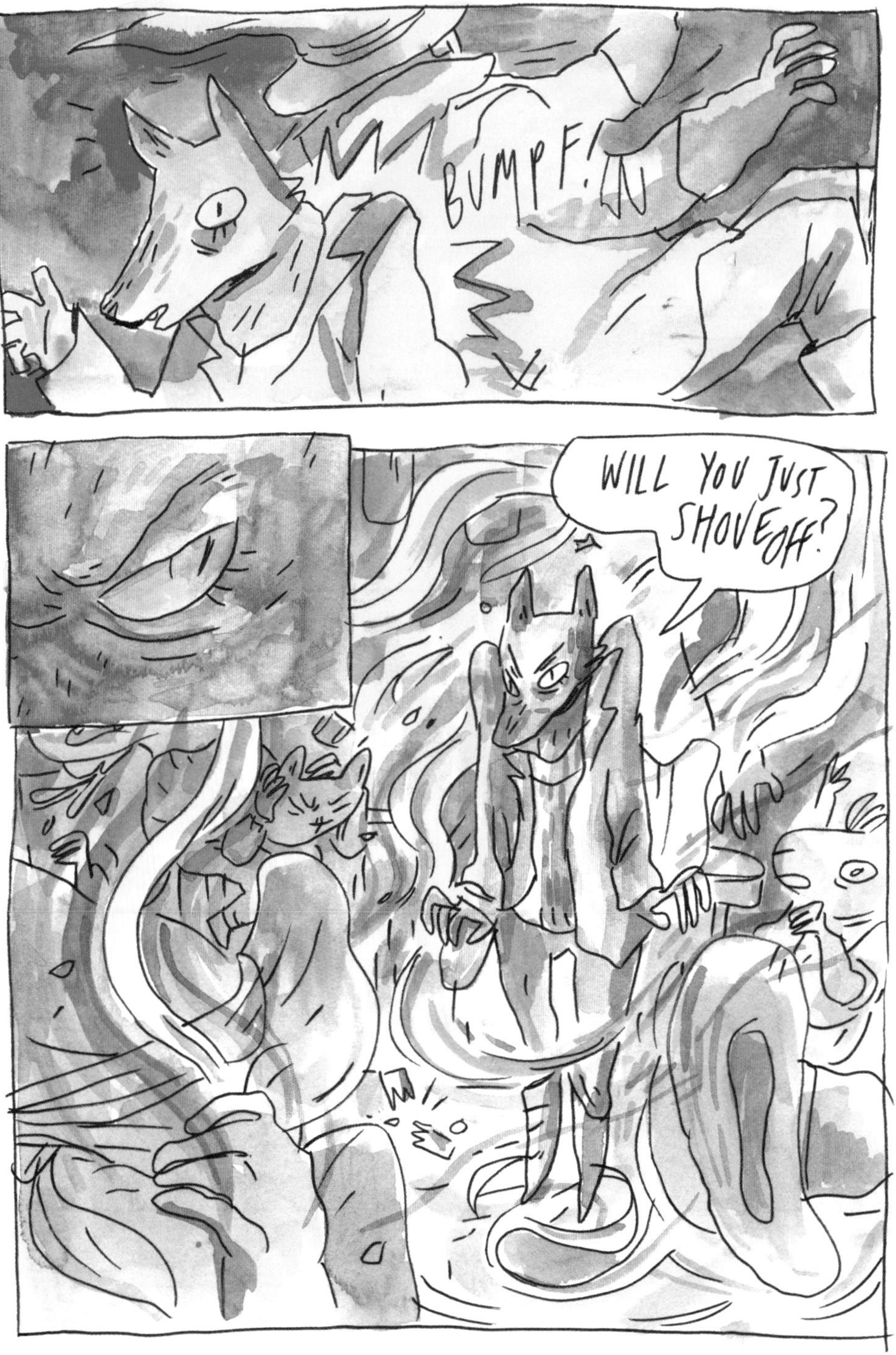
BUMPF!
WILL YOU JUST SHOVE OFF?

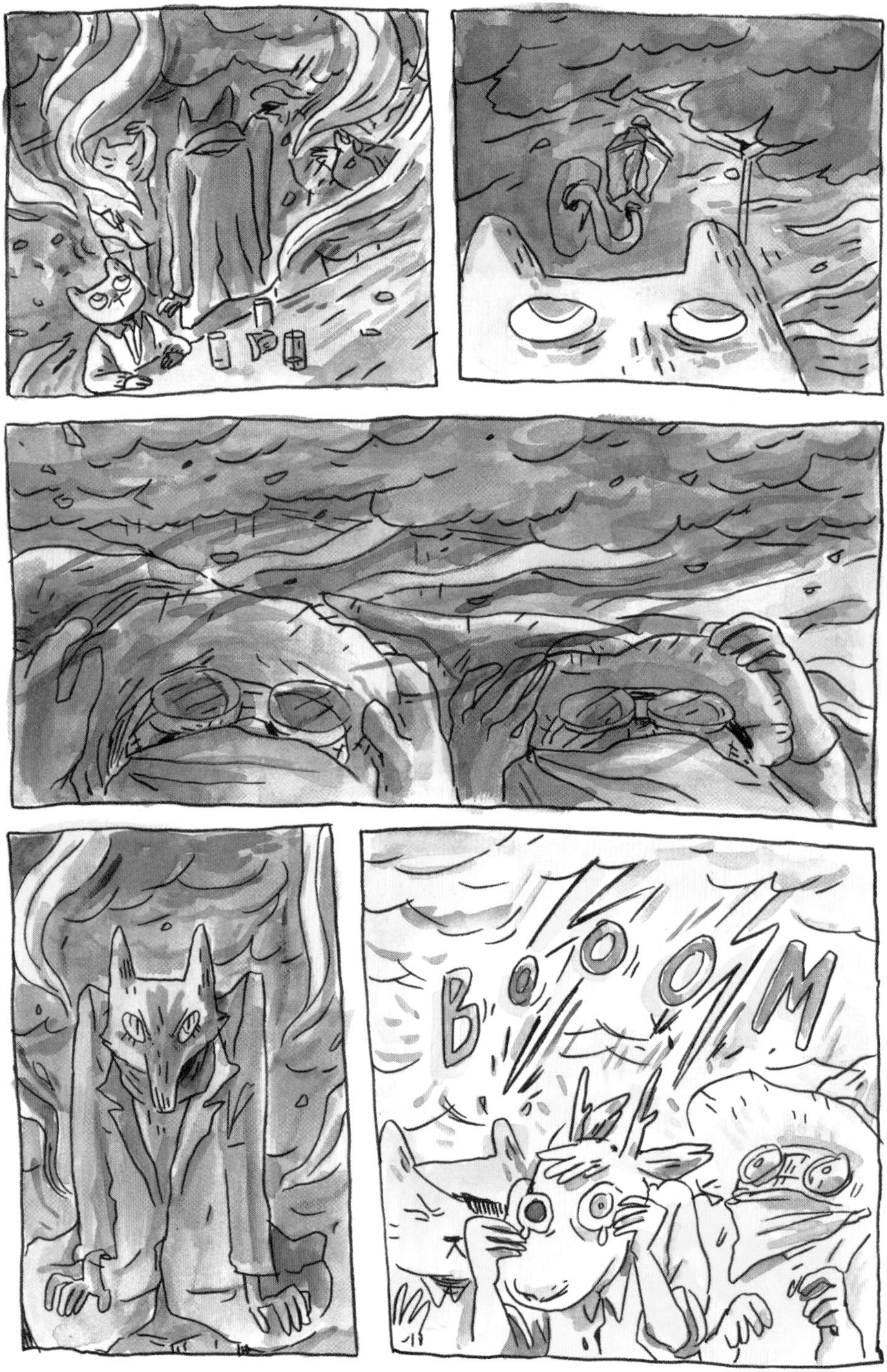
BOOOM

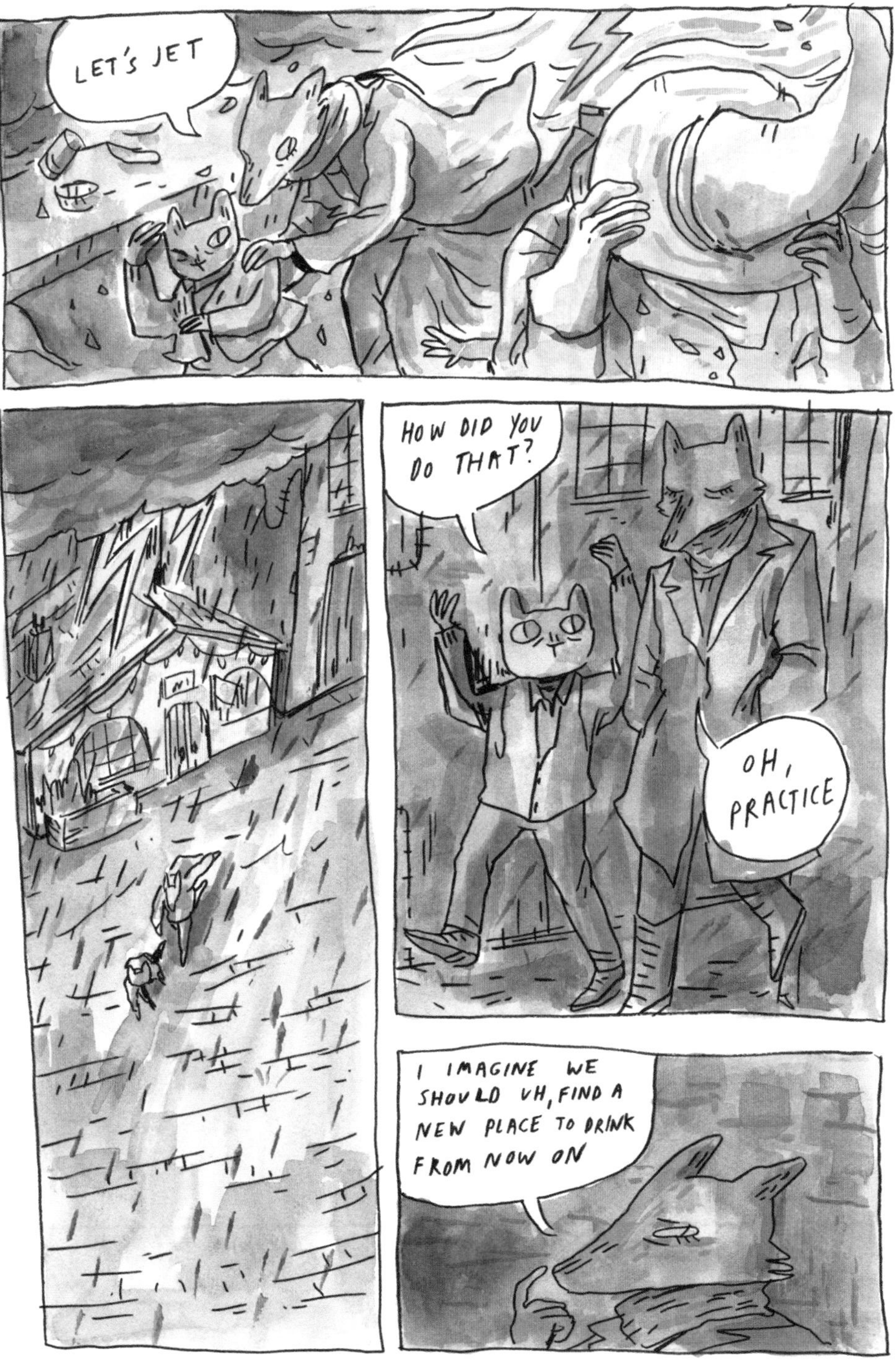
LET'S JET
HOW DID YOU DO THAT?
OH, PRACTICE
I IMAGINE WE SHOULD UH, FIND A NEW PLACE TO DRINK FROM NOW ON

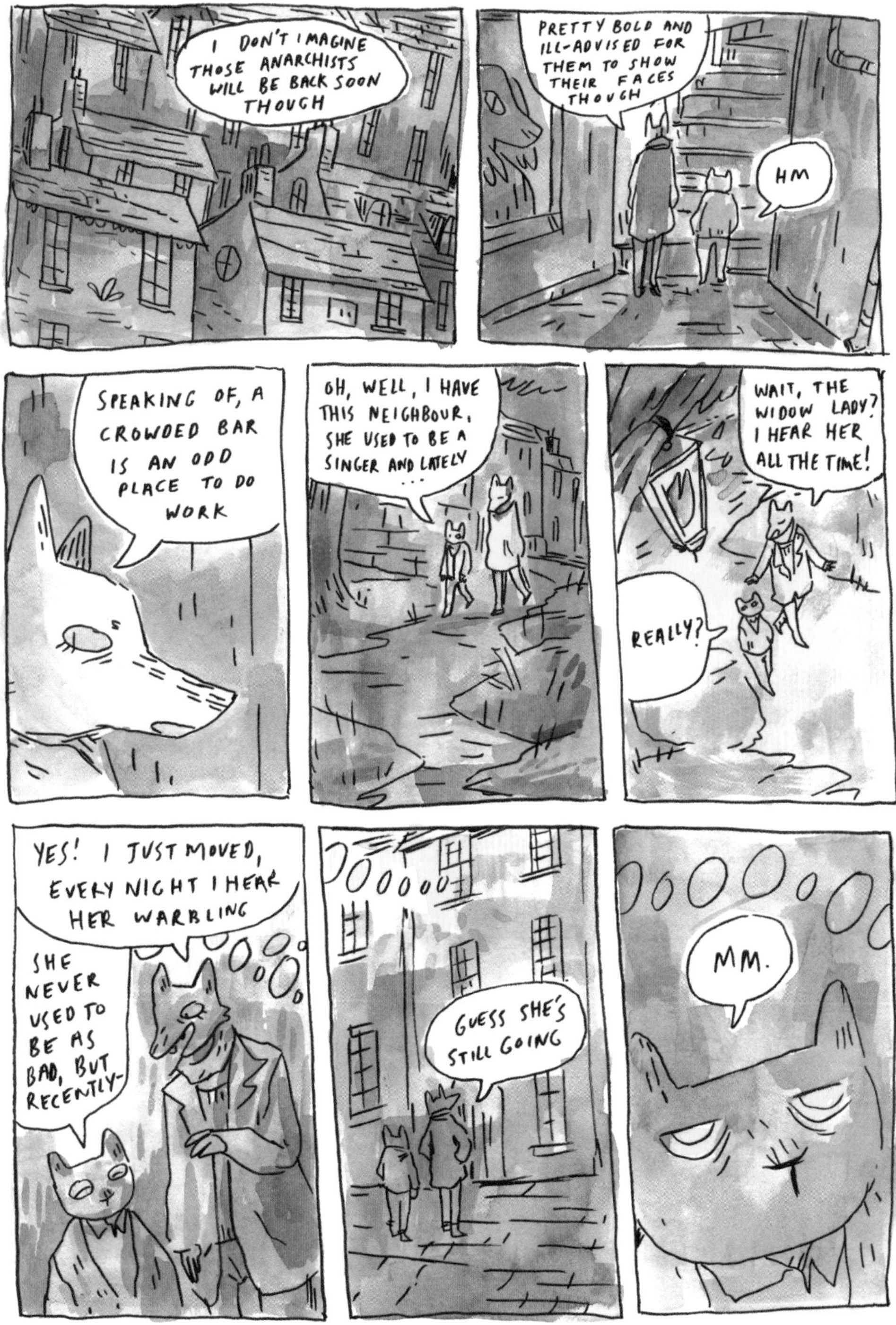
I DON'T IMAGINE THOSE ANARCHISTS WILL BE BACK SOON THOUGH
PRETTY BOLD AND ILL-ADVISED FOR THEM TO SHOW THEIR FACES THOUGH
HM
SPEAKING OF, A CROWDED BAR IS AN ODD PLACE TO DO WORK
OH, WELL, I HAVE THIS NEIGHBOUR, SHE USED TO BE A SINGER AND LATELY ...
WAIT, THE WIDOW LADY? I HEAR HER ALL THE TIME!
REALLY?
YES! I JUST MOVED, EVERY NIGHT I HEAR HER WARBLING
SHE NEVER USED TO BE AS BAD, BUT RECENTLY-
GUESS SHE'S STILL GOING
MM.

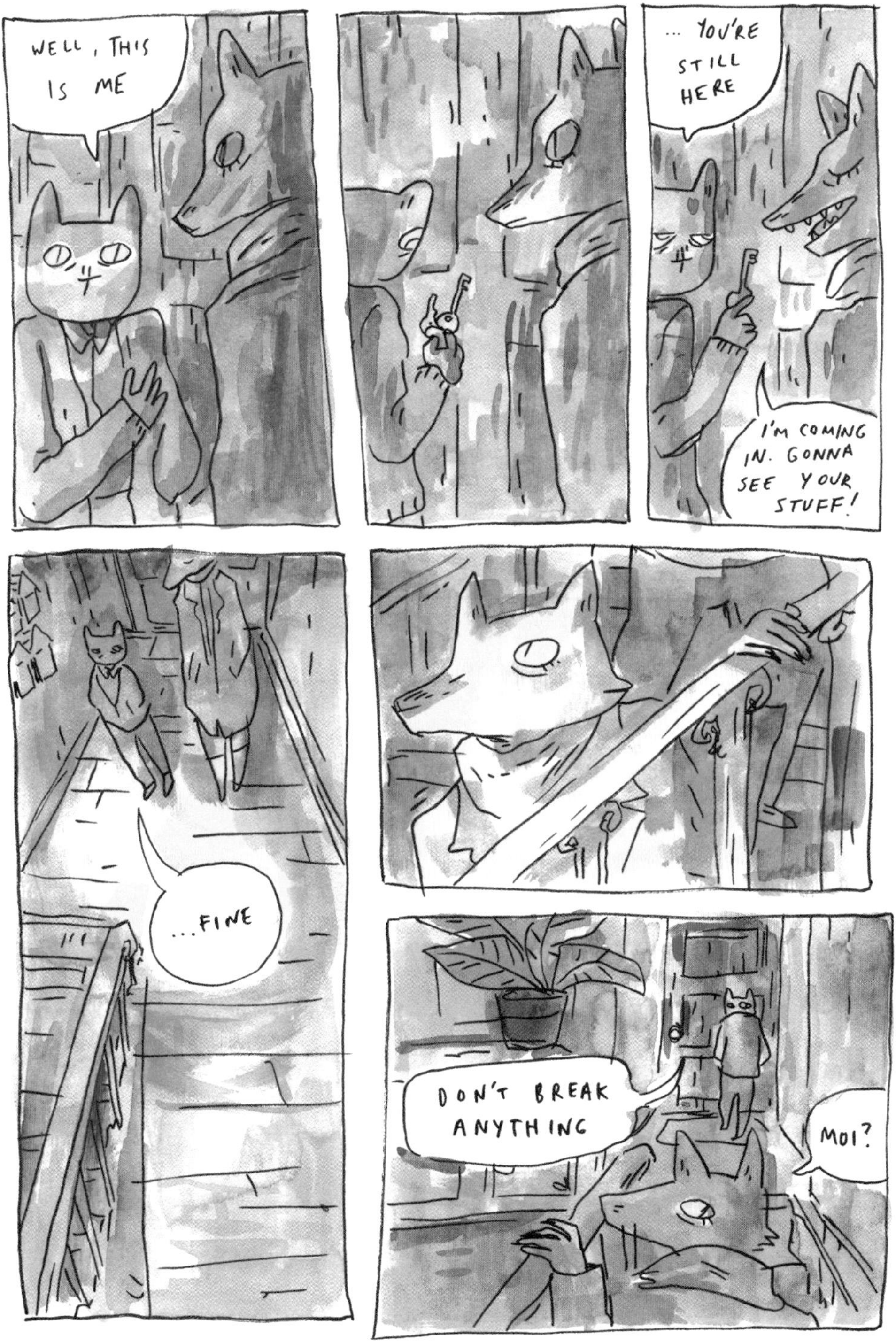
WELL, THIS IS ME
... YOU'RE STILL HERE
I'M COMING IN. GONNA SEE YOUR STUFF!
...FINE
DON'T BREAK ANYTHING
MOI?

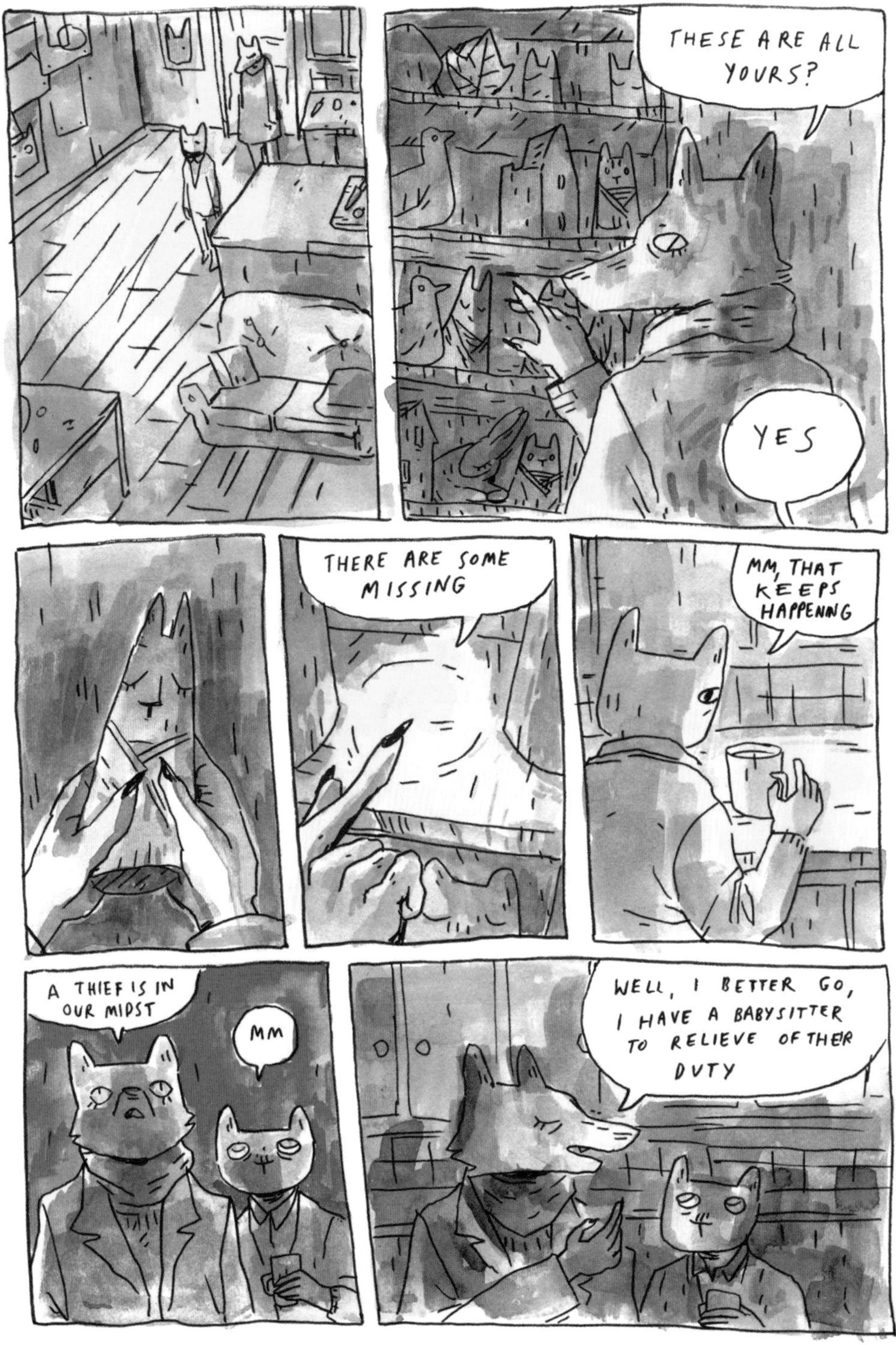
THESE ARE ALL YOURS?
YES
THERE ARE SOME MISSING
MM, THAT KEEPS HAPPENING
A THIEF IS IN OUR MIDST
MM
WELL, I BETTER GO, I HAVE A BABYSITTER TO RELIEVE OF THEIR DUTY

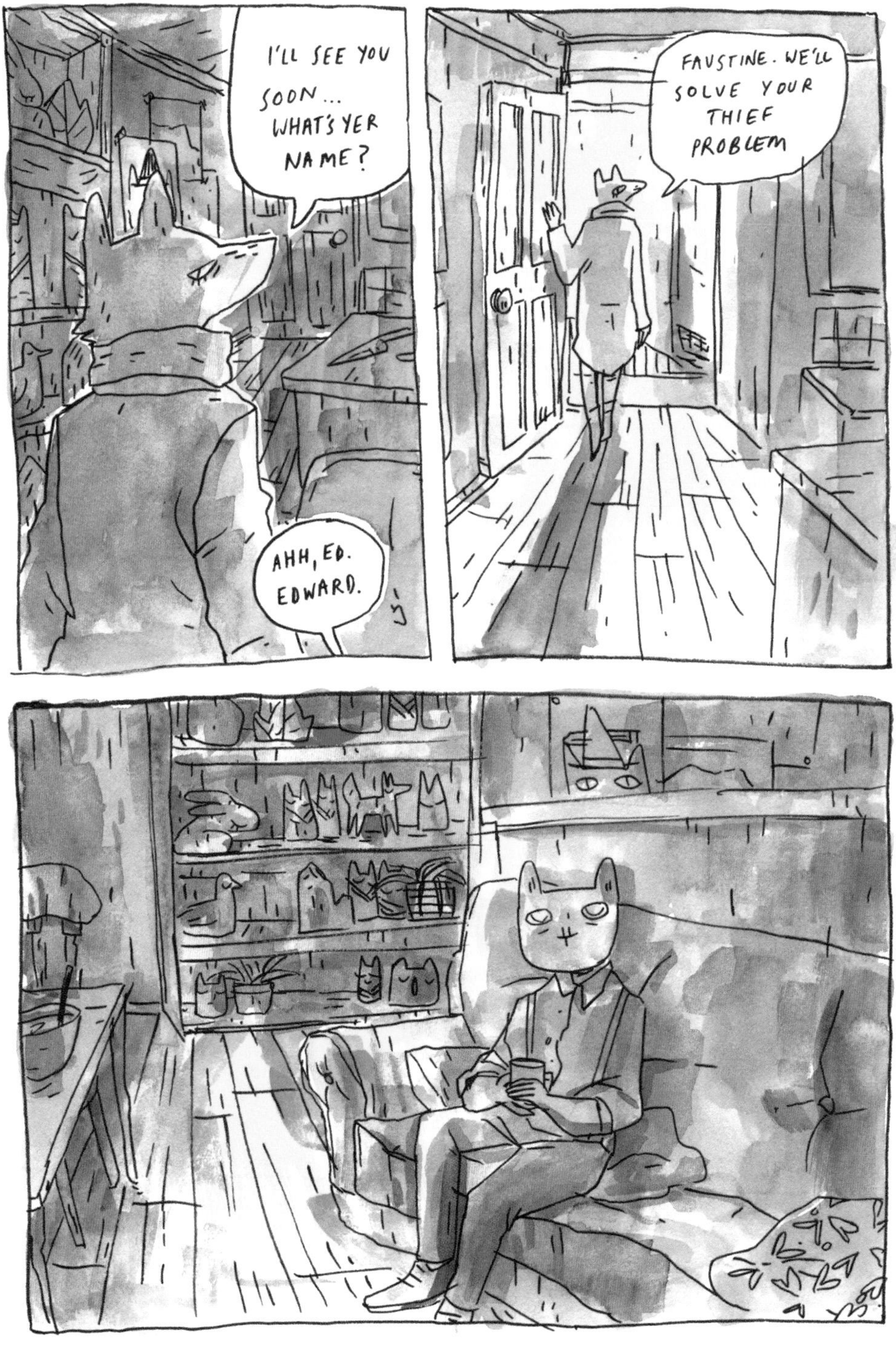
I'LL SEE YOU SOON... WHAT'S YER NAME?
AHH, ED. EDWARD.
FAUSTINE. WE'LL SOLVE YOUR THIEF PROBLEM

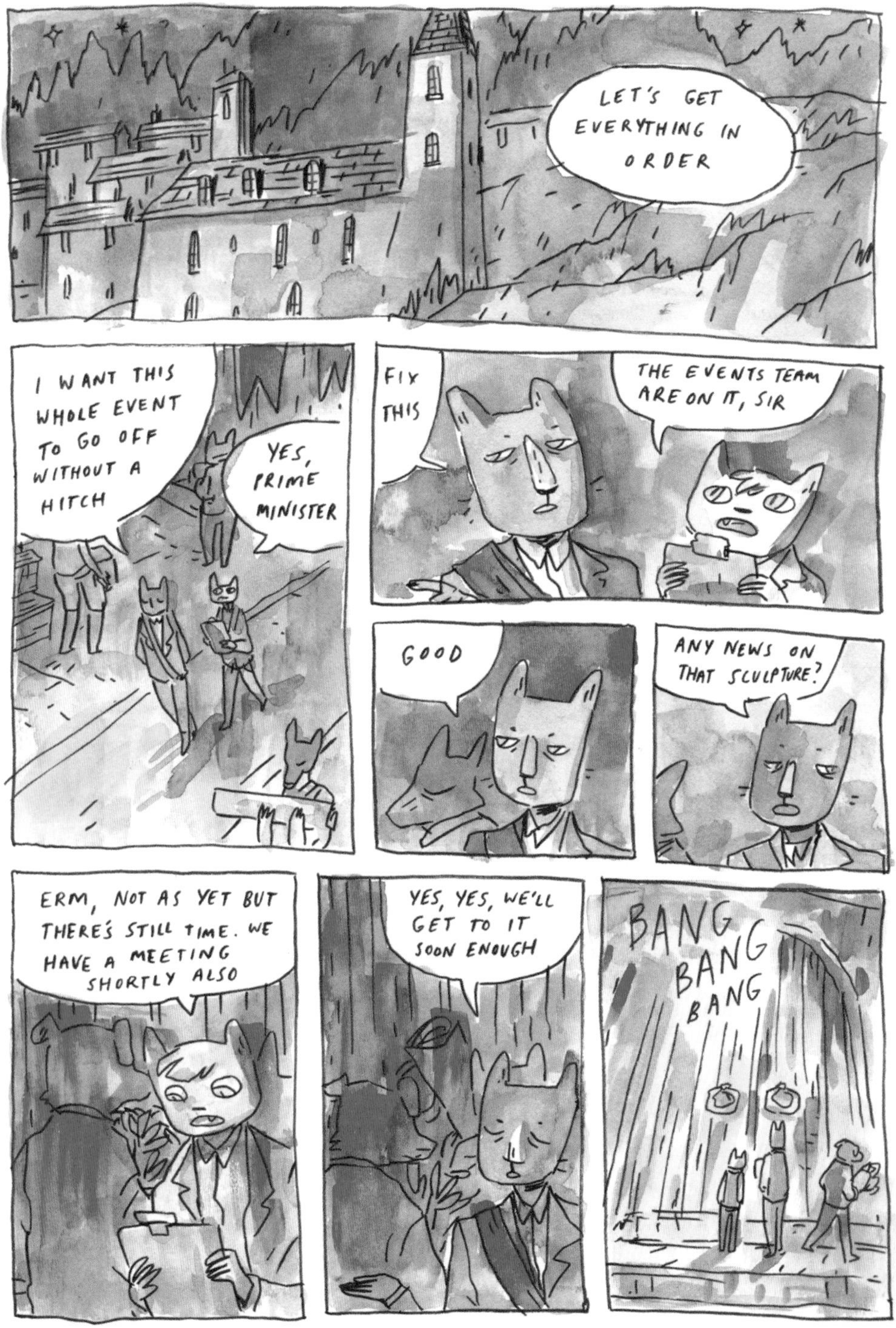
LET'S GET EVERYTHING IN ORDER
I WANT THIS WHOLE EVENT TO GO OFF WITHOUT A HITCH
YES, PRIME MINISTER
FIX THIS
THE EVENTS TEAM ARE ON IT, SIR
GOOD
ANY NEWS ON THAT SCULPTURE?
ERM, NOT AS YET BUT THERE'S STILL TIME. WE HAVE A MEETING SHORTLY ALSO
YES, YES, WE'LL GET TO IT SOON ENOUGH
BANG
BANG
BANG

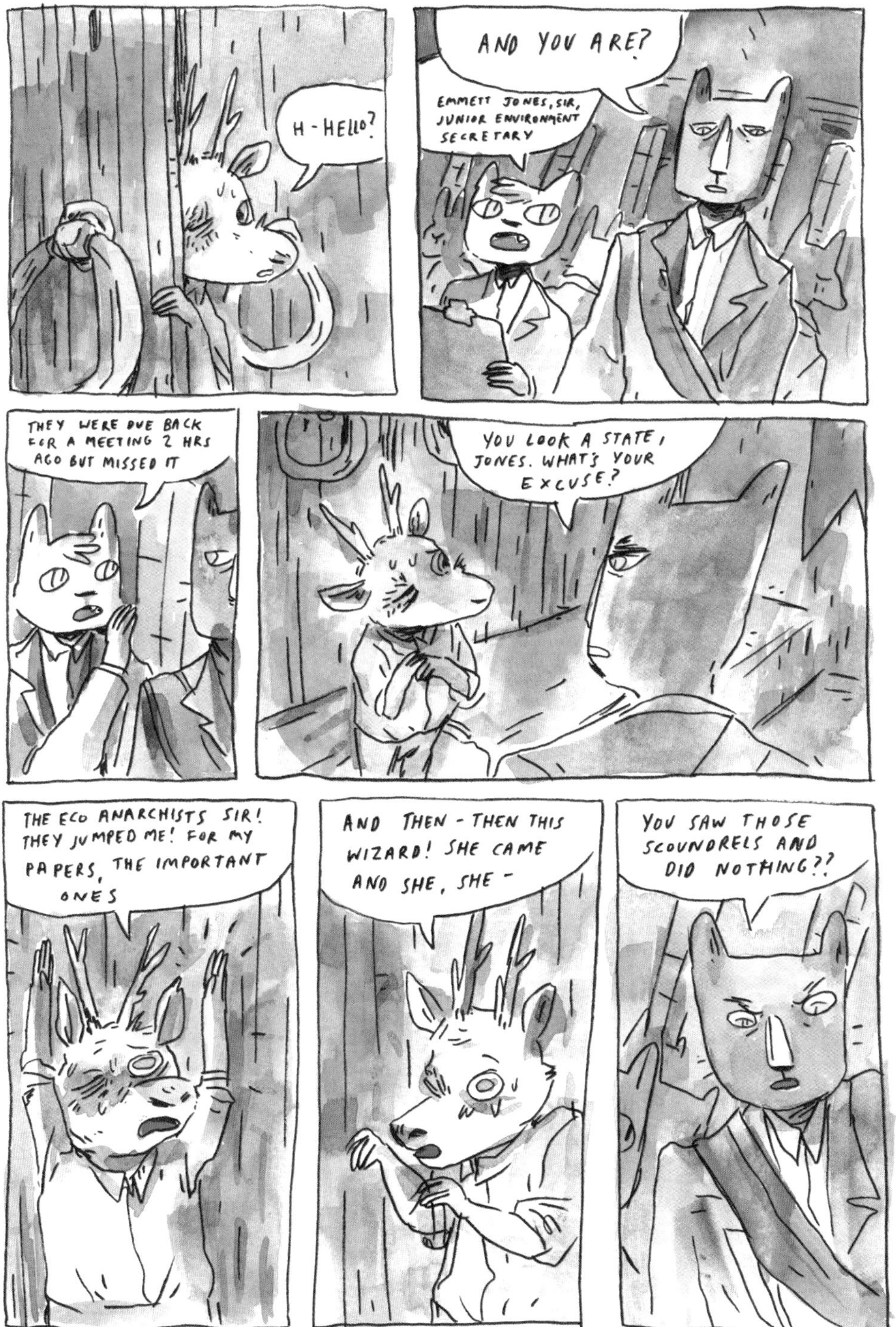
H-HELLO?
AND YOU ARE?
EMMETT JONES, SIR, JUNIOR ENVIRONMENT SECRETARY
THEY WERE DUE BACK FOR A MEETING 2 HRS AGO BUT MISSED IT
YOU LOOK A STATE, JONES. WHAT'S YOUR EXCUSE?
THE ECO ANARCHISTS SIR! THEY JUMPED ME! FOR MY PAPERS, THE IMPORTANT ONES
AND THEN - THEN THIS WIZARD! SHE CAME AND SHE, SHE -
YOU SAW THOSE SCOUNDRELS AND DID NOTHING??

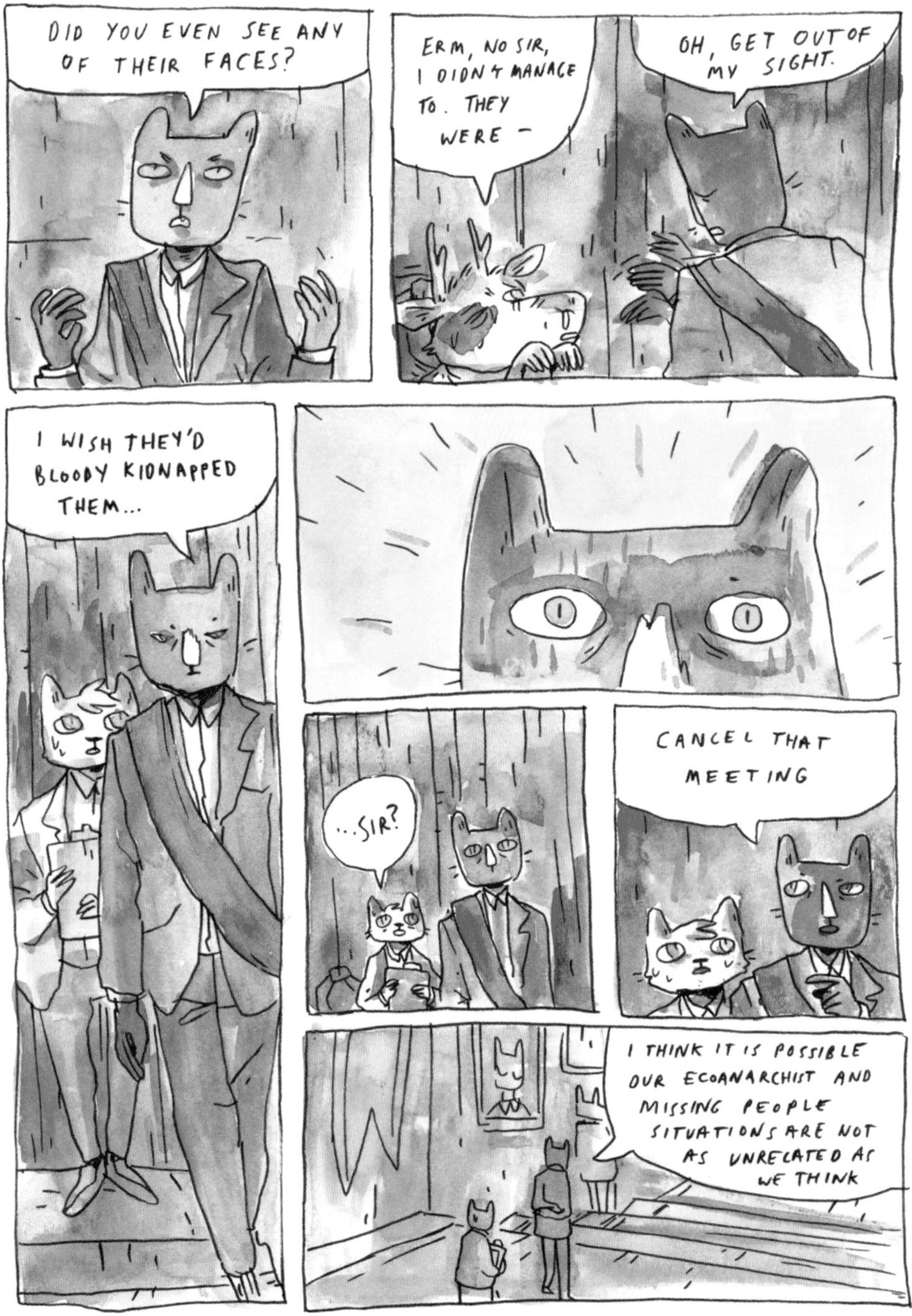
DID YOU EVEN SEE ANY OF THEIR FACES?
ERM, NO SIR, I DIDN'T MANAGE TO. THEY WERE -
OH, GET OUT OF MY SIGHT.
I WISH THEY'D BLOODY KIDNAPPED THEM...
...SIR?
CANCEL THAT MEETING
I THINK IT IS POSSIBLE OUR ECOANARCHIST AND MISSING PEOPLE SITUATIONS ARE NOT AS UNRELATED AS WE THINK

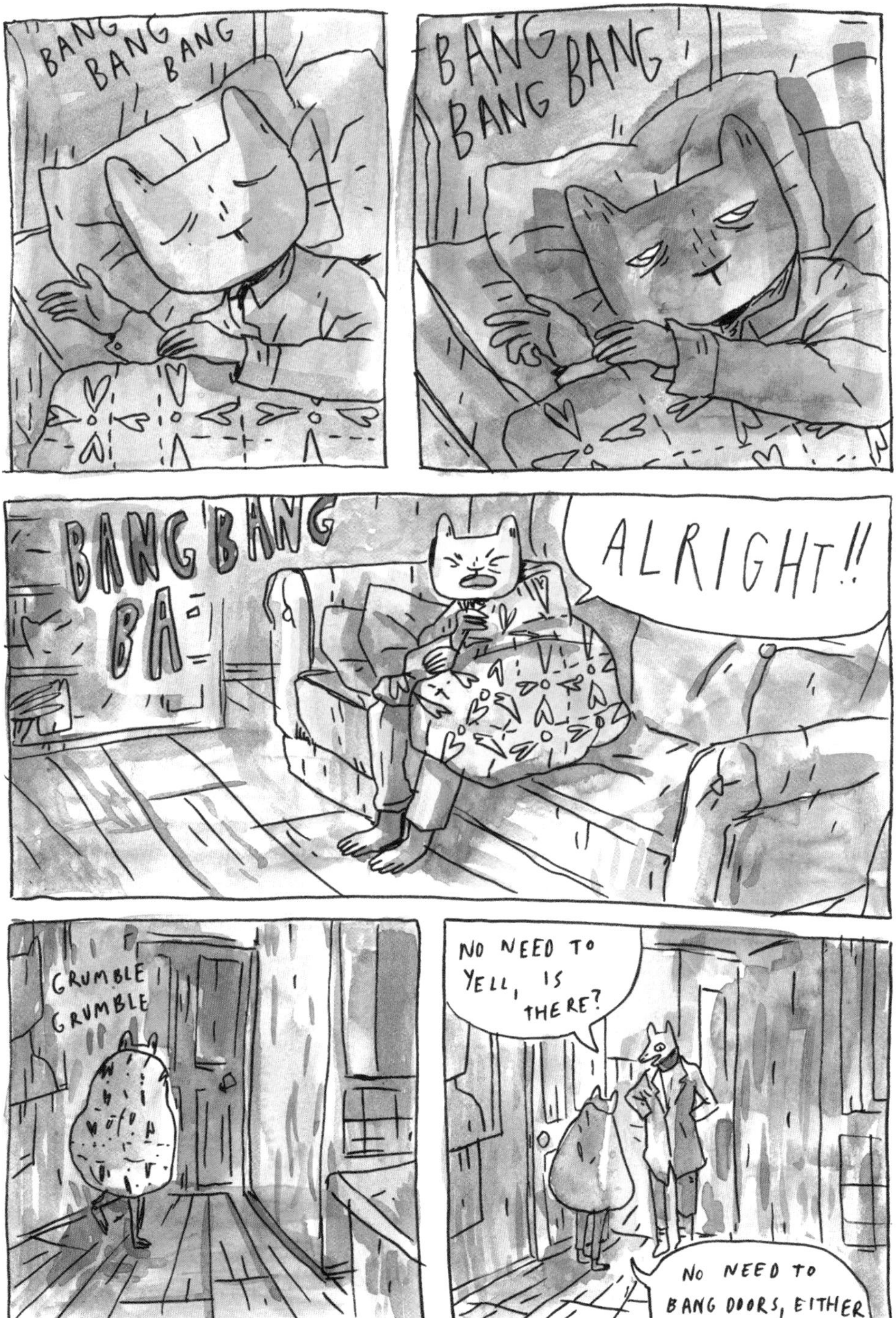
BANG BANG BANG
BANG BANG BANG
BANG BANG BA
ALRIGHT!!
GRUMBLE GRUMBLE
NO NEED TO YELL, IS THERE?
NO NEED TO BANG DOORS, EITHER

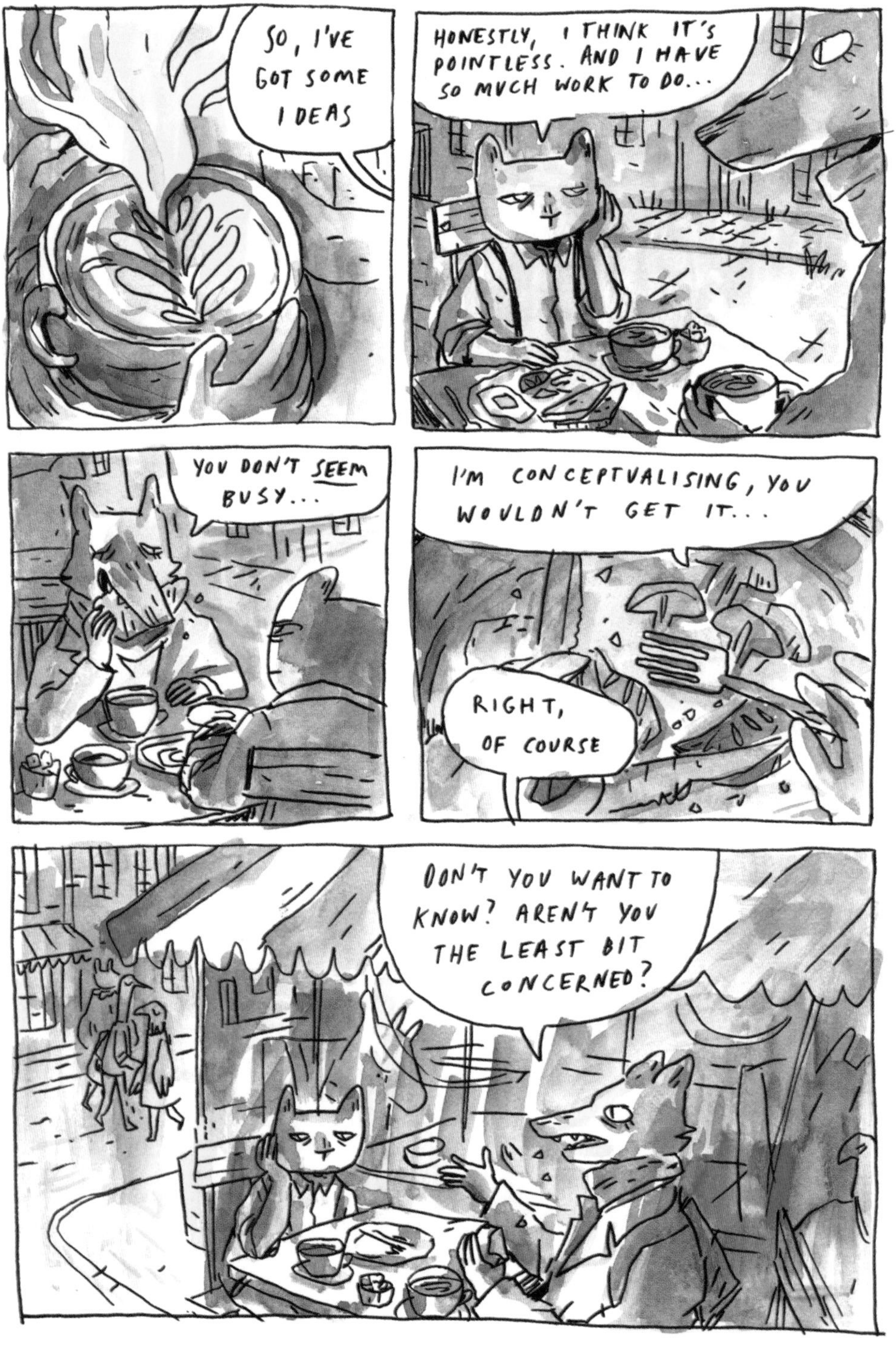
SO, I'VE GOT SOME IDEAS
HONESTLY, I THINK IT'S POINTLESS. AND I HAVE SO MUCH WORK TO DO...
YOU DON'T SEEM BUSY...
I'M CONCEPTUALISING, YOU WOULDN'T GET IT...
RIGHT, OF COURSE
DON'T YOU WANT TO KNOW? AREN'T YOU THE LEAST BIT CONCERNED?

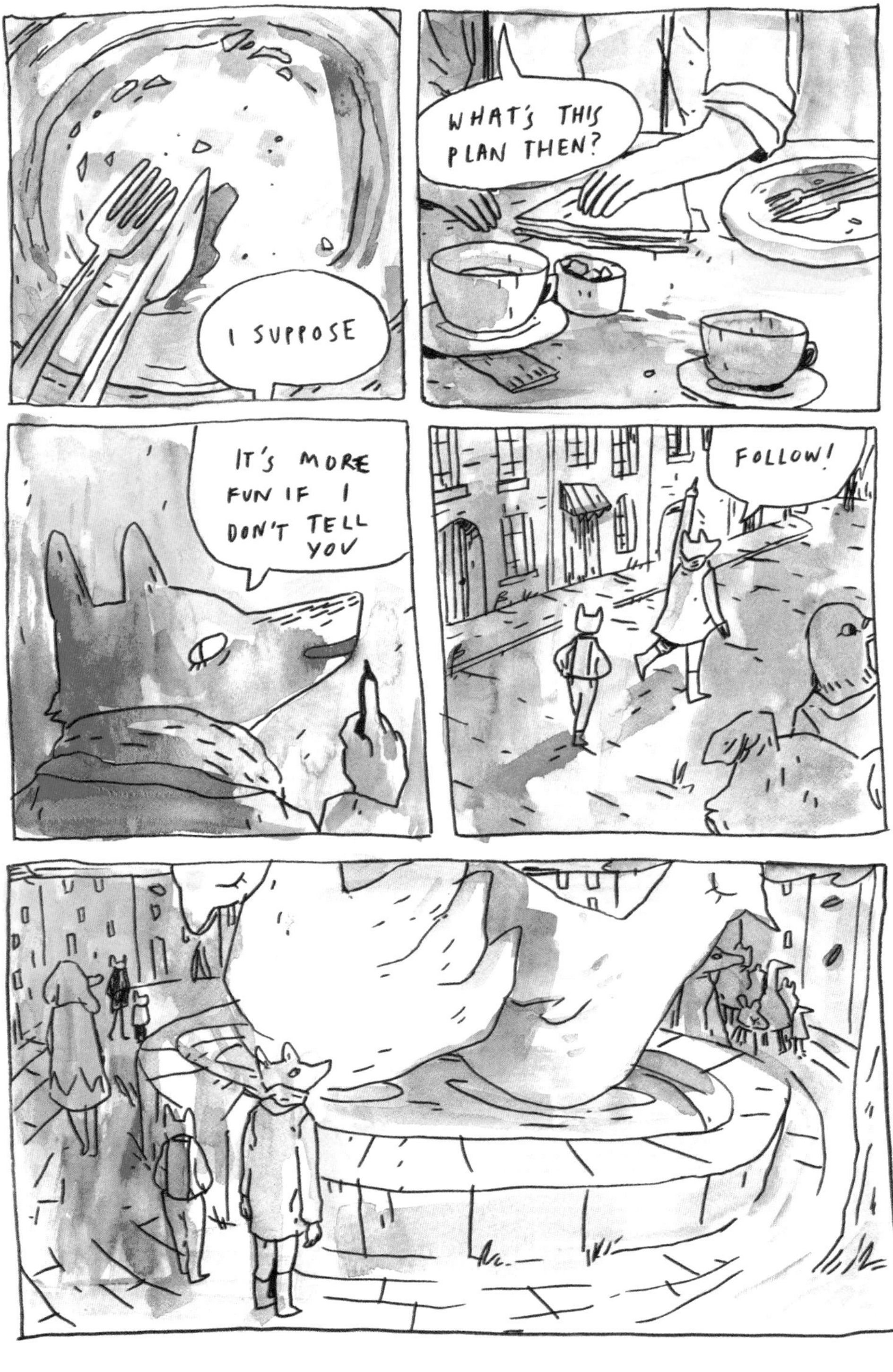
I SUPPOSE
WHAT'S THIS PLAN THEN?
IT'S MORE FUN IF I DON'T TELL YOU
FOLLOW!

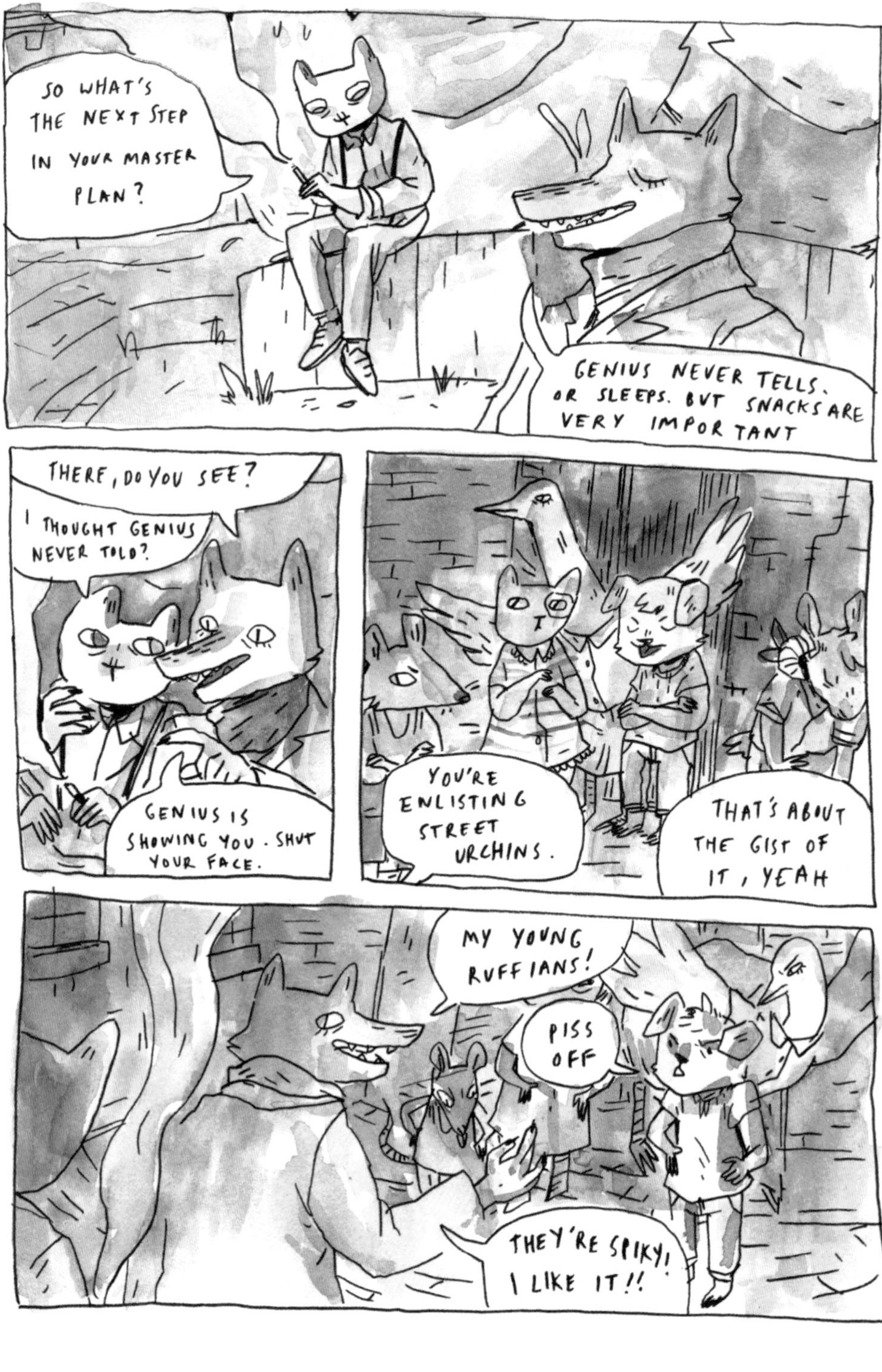
SO WHAT'S THE NEXT STEP IN YOUR MASTER PLAN?
GENIUS NEVER TELLS. OR SLEEPS. BUT SNACKS ARE VERY IMPORTANT
THERE, DO YOU SEE?
I THOUGHT GENIUS NEVER TOLD?
GENIUS IS SHOWING YOU. SHUT YOUR FACE.
YOU'RE ENLISTING STREET URCHINS.
THAT'S ABOUT THE GIST OF IT, YEAH
MY YOUNG RUFFIANS!
PISS OFF
THEY'RE SPIKY! I LIKE IT!!

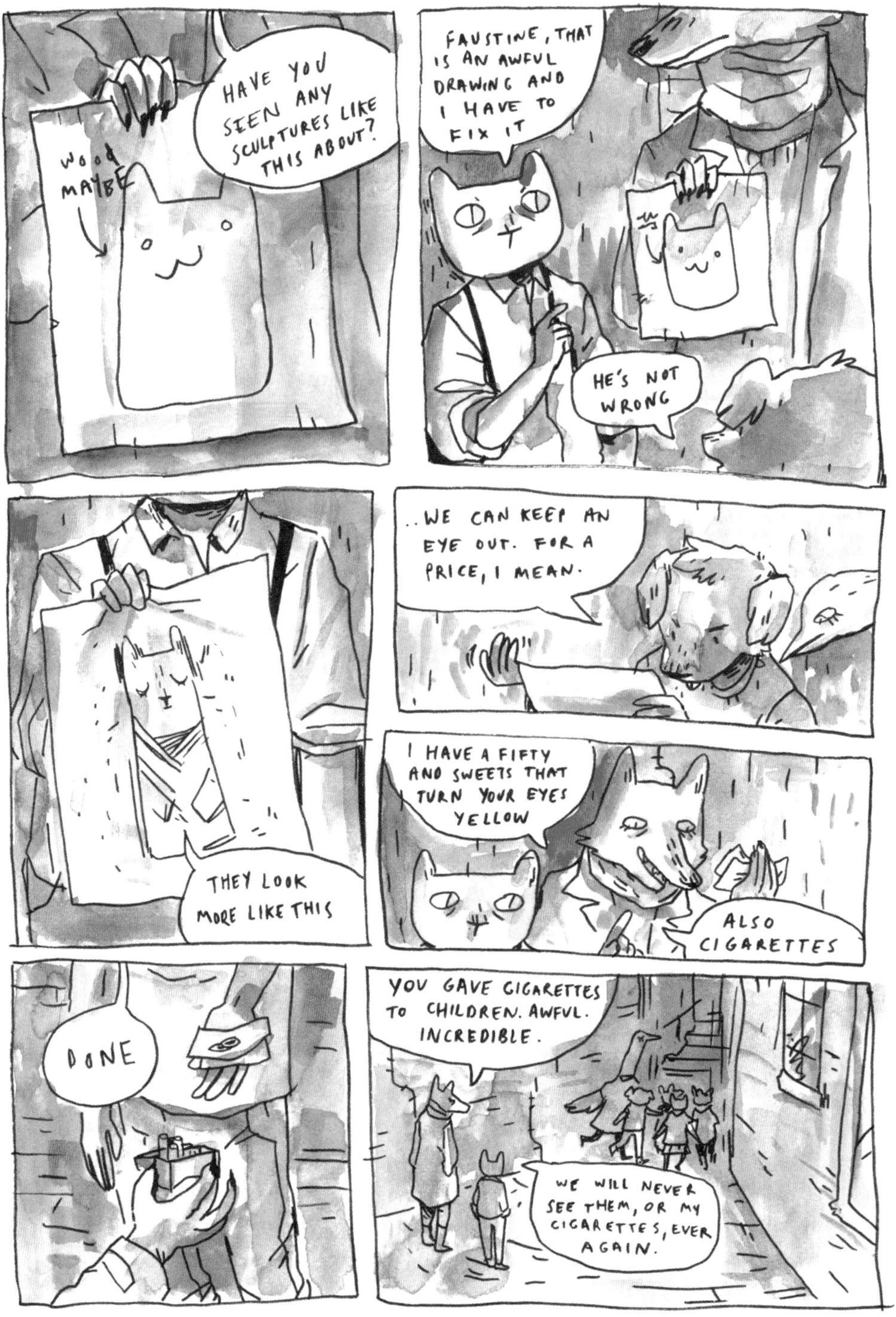
WOOD MAYBE
HAVE YOU SEEN ANY SCULPTURES LIKE THIS ABOUT?
FAUSTINE, THAT IS AN AWFUL DRAWING AND I HAVE TO FIX IT
HE'S NOT WRONG
THEY LOOK MORE LIKE THIS
..WE CAN KEEP AN EYE OUT. FOR A PRICE, I MEAN.
I HAVE A FIFTY AND SWEETS THAT TURN YOUR EYES YELLOW
ALSO CIGARETTES
DONE
YOU GAVE CIGARETTES TO CHILDREN. AWFUL. INCREDIBLE.
WE WILL NEVER SEE THEM, OR MY CIGARETTES, EVER AGAIN.

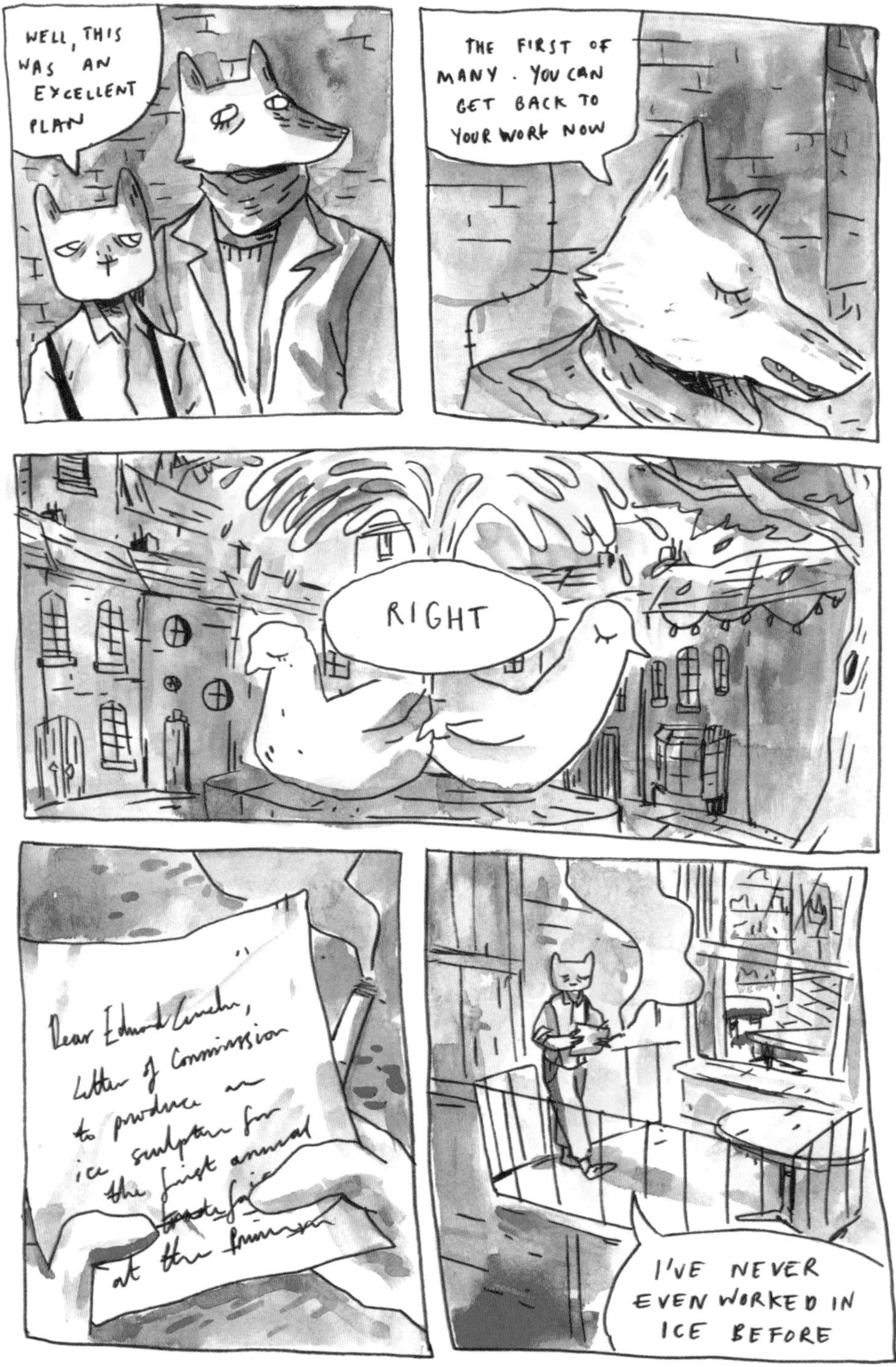
WELL, THIS WAS AN EXCELLENT PLAN
THE FIRST OF MANY. YOU CAN GET BACK TO YOUR WORK NOW
RIGHT
Dear Edmund
Letter of Commission
to produce an
ice sculpture for
the first annual
I'VE NEVER EVEN WORKED IN ICE BEFORE

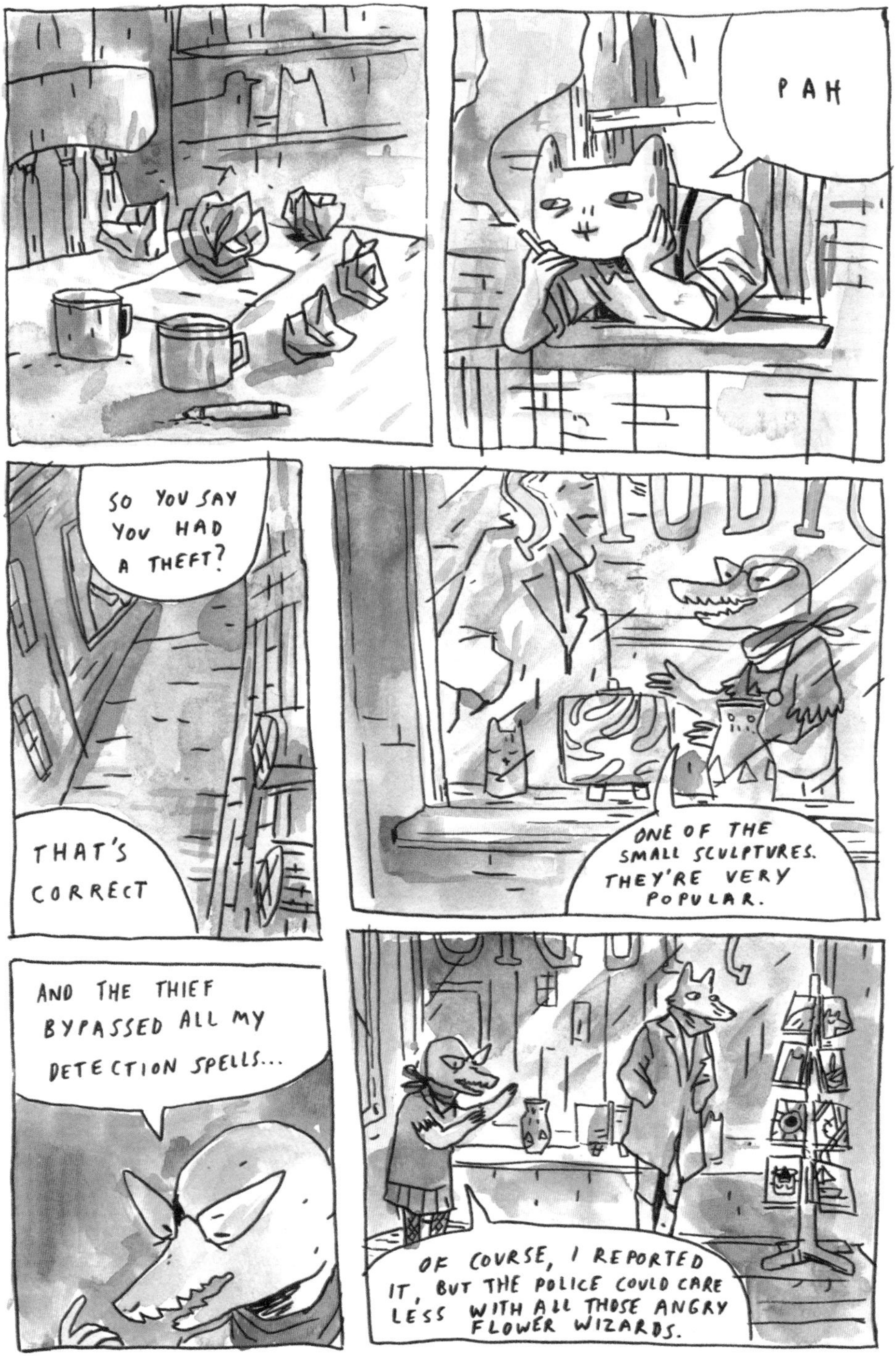
PAH
SO YOU SAY YOU HAD A THEFT?
THAT'S CORRECT
ONE OF THE SMALL SCULPTURES. THEY'RE VERY POPULAR.
AND THE THIEF BYPASSED ALL MY DETECTION SPELLS...
OF COURSE, I REPORTED IT, BUT THE POLICE COULD CARE LESS WITH ALL THOSE ANGRY FLOWER WIZARDS.

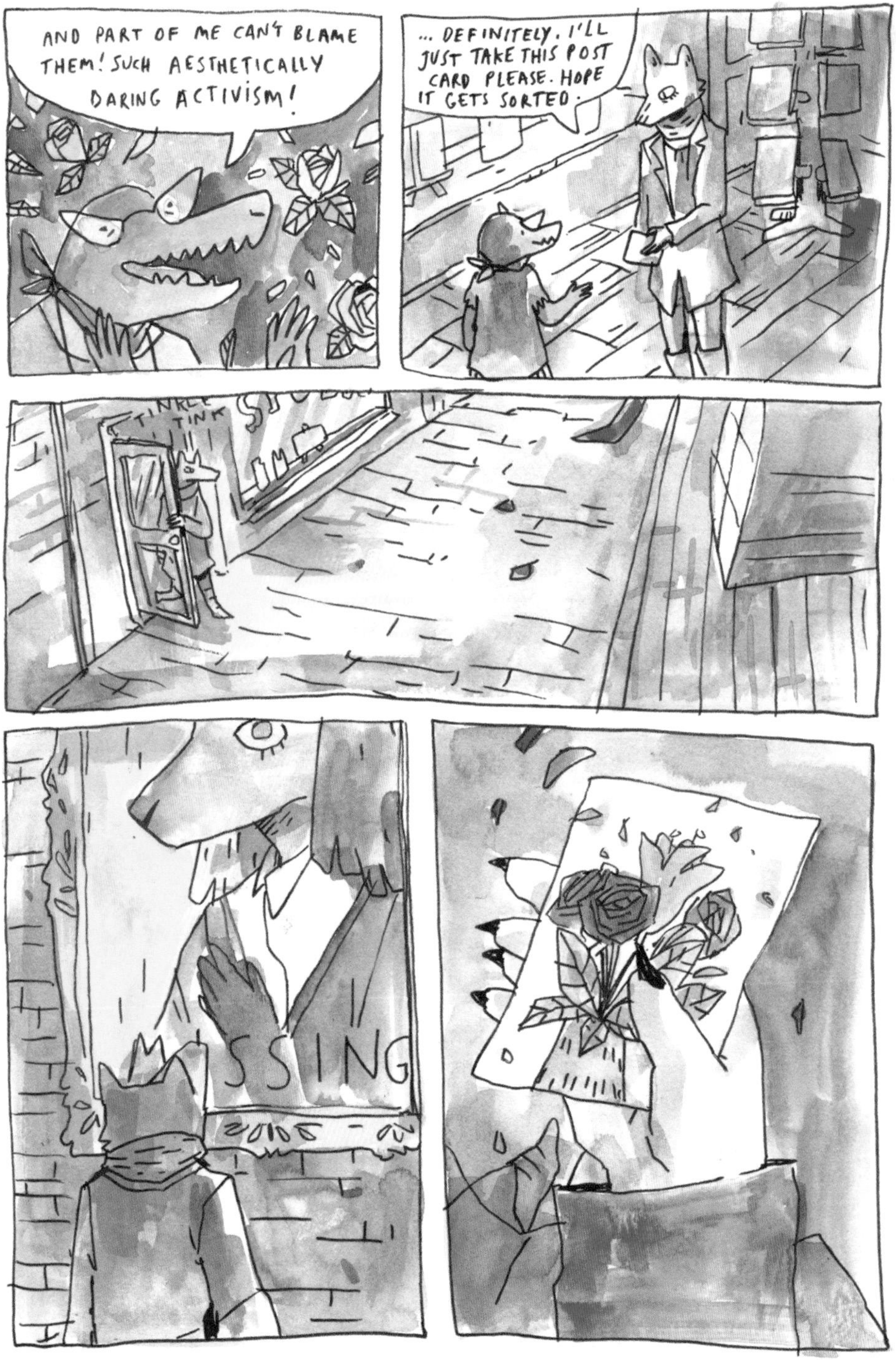
AND PART OF ME CAN'T BLAME THEM! SUCH AESTHETICALLY DARING ACTIVISM!
... DEFINITELY. I'LL JUST TAKE THIS POST CARD PLEASE. HOPE IT GETS SORTED.
TINKLE TINK
SSING

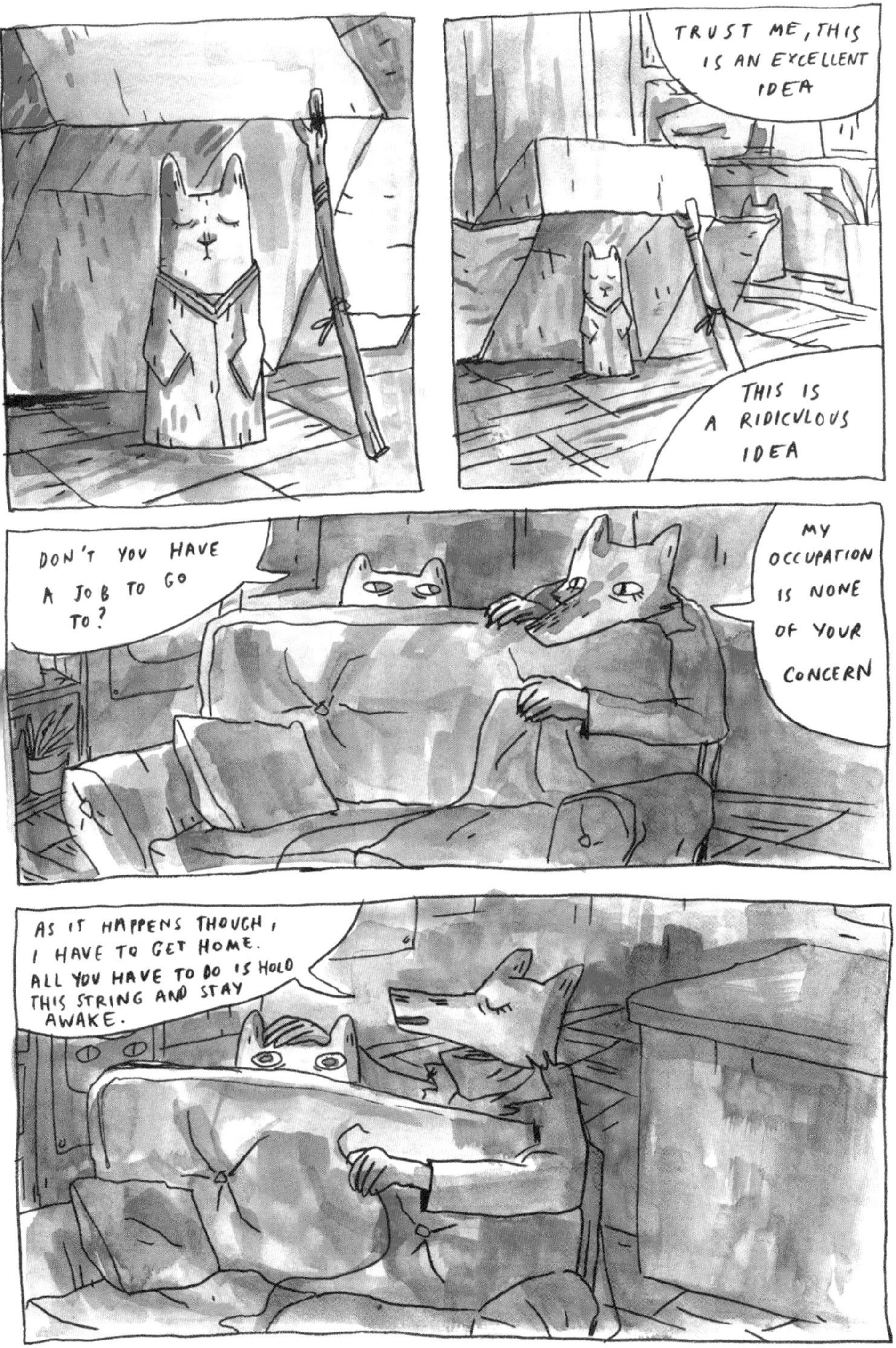
TRUST ME, THIS IS AN EXCELLENT IDEA
THIS IS A RIDICULOUS IDEA
DON'T YOU HAVE A JOB TO GO TO?
MY OCCUPATION IS NONE OF YOUR CONCERN
AS IT HAPPENS THOUGH, I HAVE TO GET HOME. ALL YOU HAVE TO DO IS HOLD THIS STRING AND STAY AWAKE.

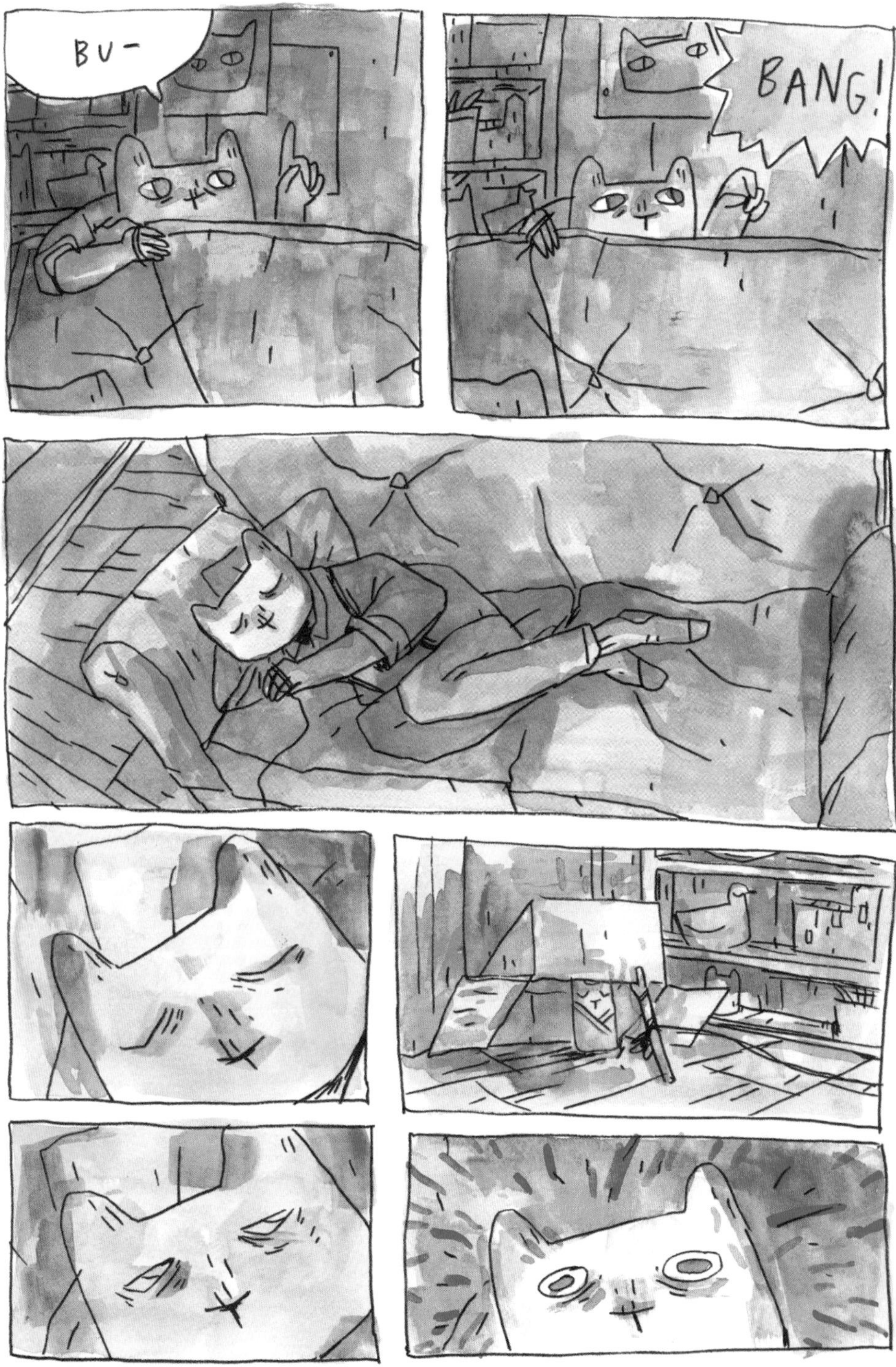
BU-
BANG!

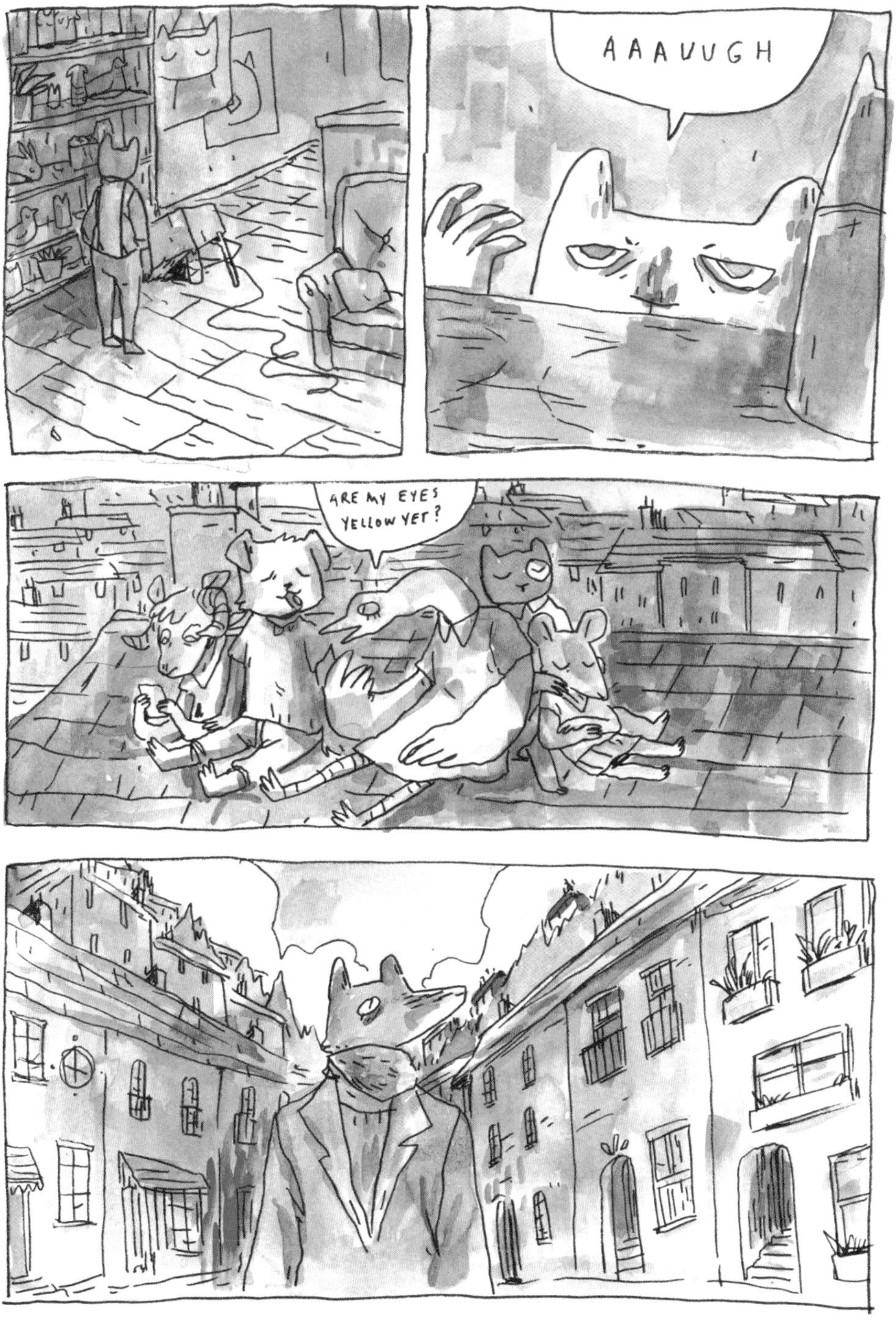
AAAUUGH
ARE MY EYES YELLOW YET?

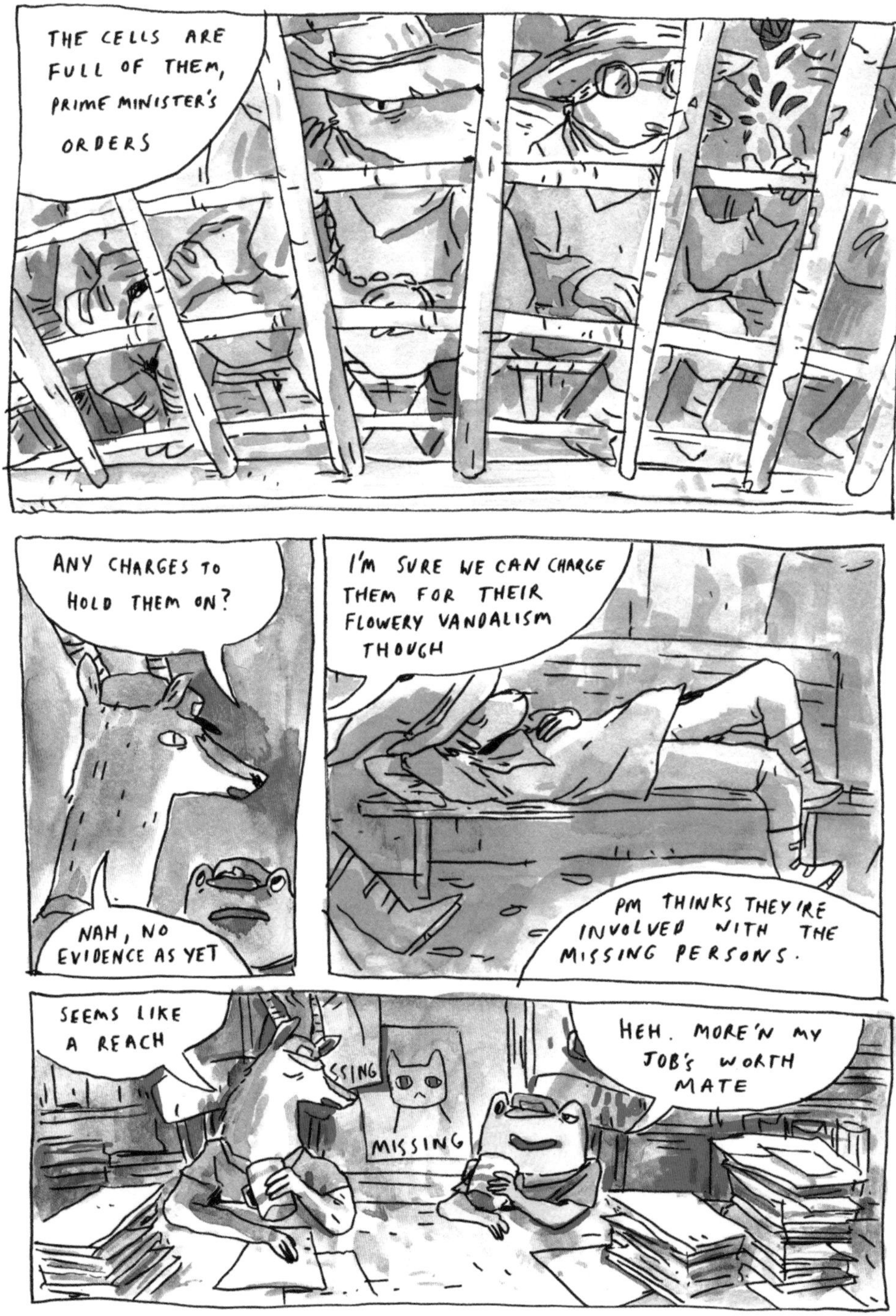
THE CELLS ARE FULL OF THEM, PRIME MINISTER'S ORDERS
ANY CHARGES TO HOLD THEM ON?
NAH, NO EVIDENCE AS YET
I'M SURE WE CAN CHARGE THEM FOR THEIR FLOWERY VANDALISM THOUGH
PM THINKS THEY'RE INVOLVED WITH THE MISSING PERSONS.
SEEMS LIKE A REACH
SSING
MISSING
HEH. MORE'N MY JOB'S WORTH MATE

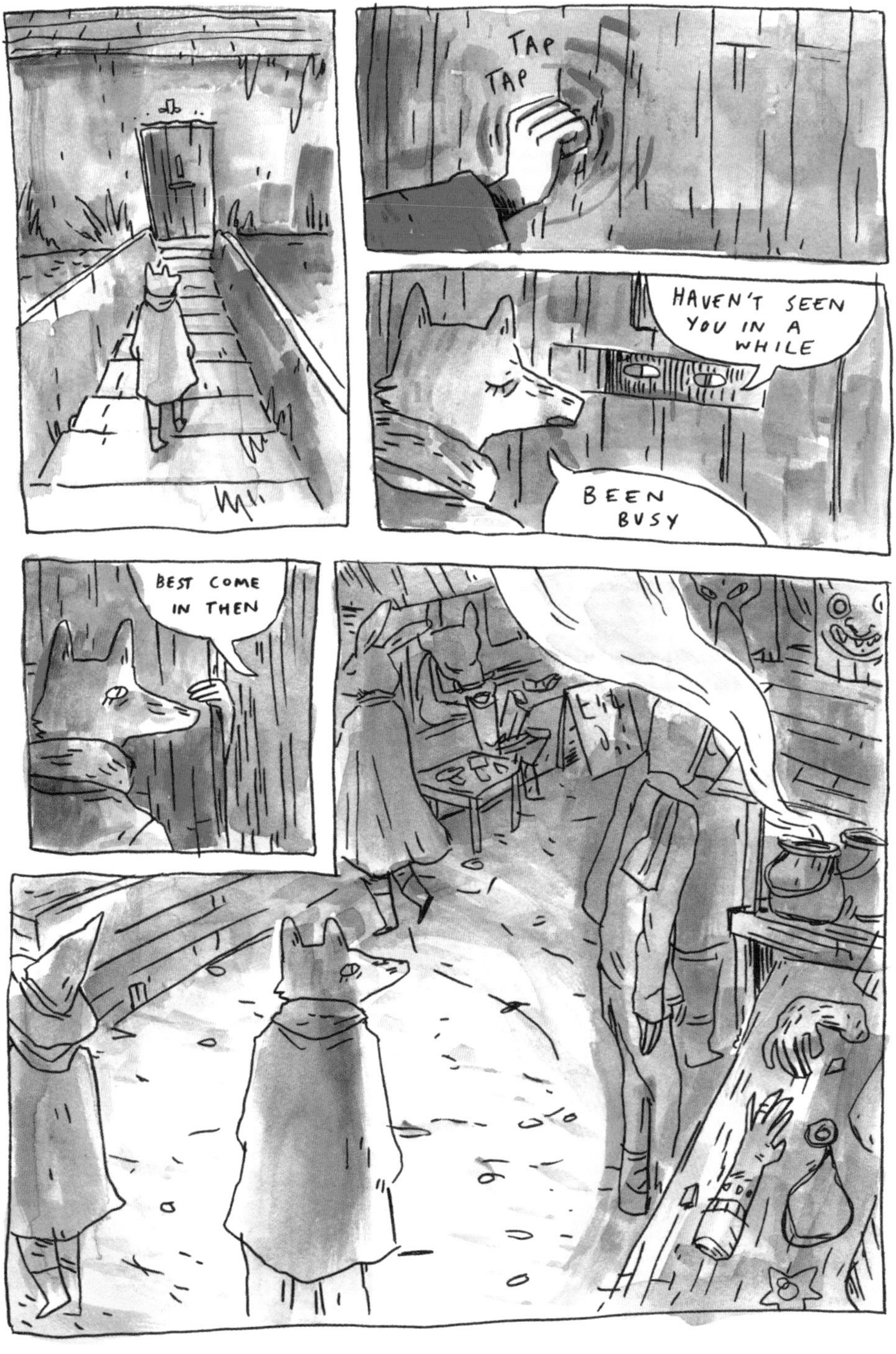
TAP
TAP
HAVEN'T SEEN YOU IN A WHILE
BEEN BUSY
BEST COME IN THEN

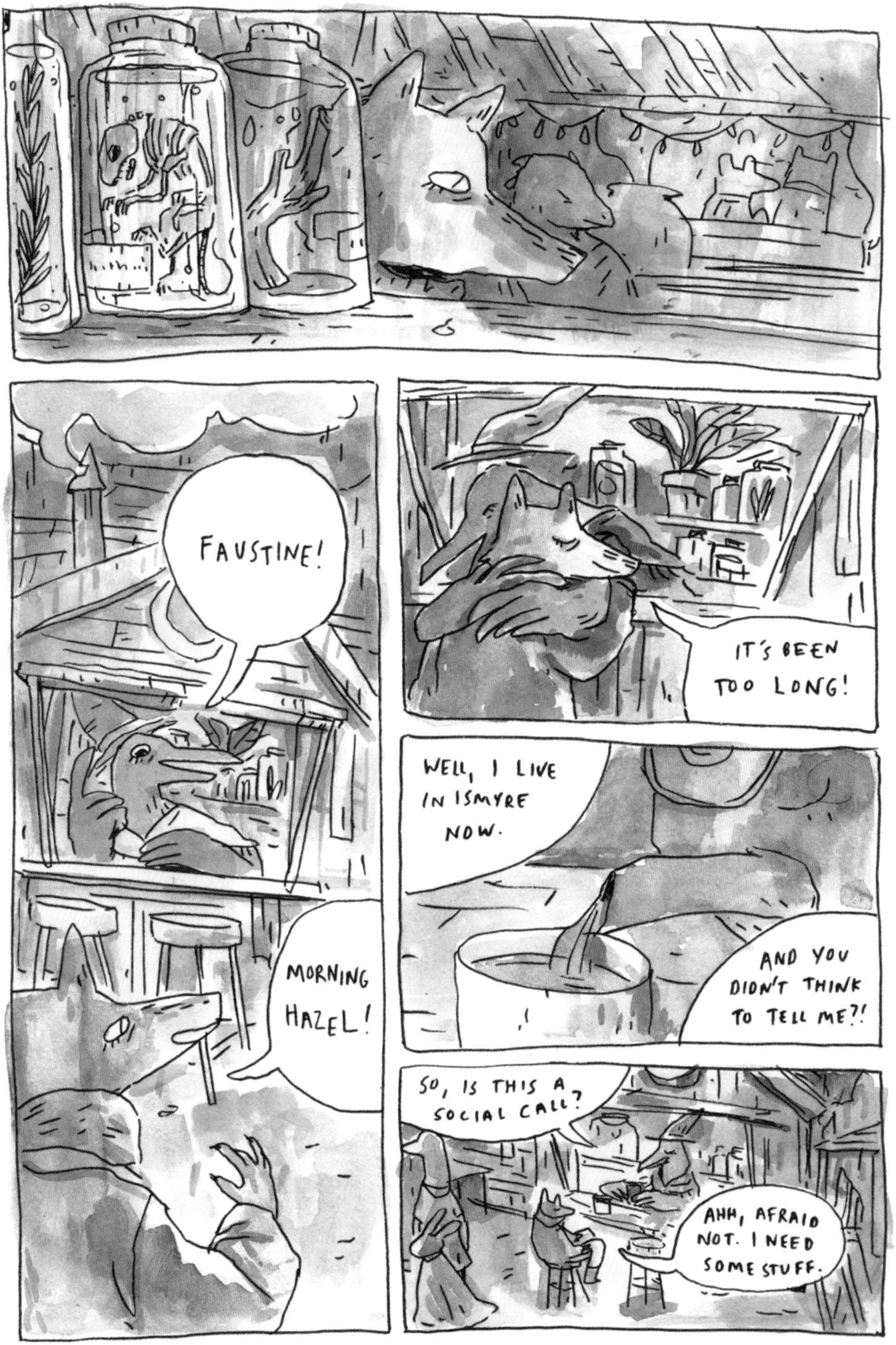
FAUSTINE!
IT'S BEEN TOO LONG!
WELL, I LIVE IN ISMYRE NOW.
AND YOU DIDN'T THINK TO TELL ME?!
MORNING HAZEL!
SO, IS THIS A SOCIAL CALL?
AHH, AFRAID NOT. I NEED SOME STUFF.

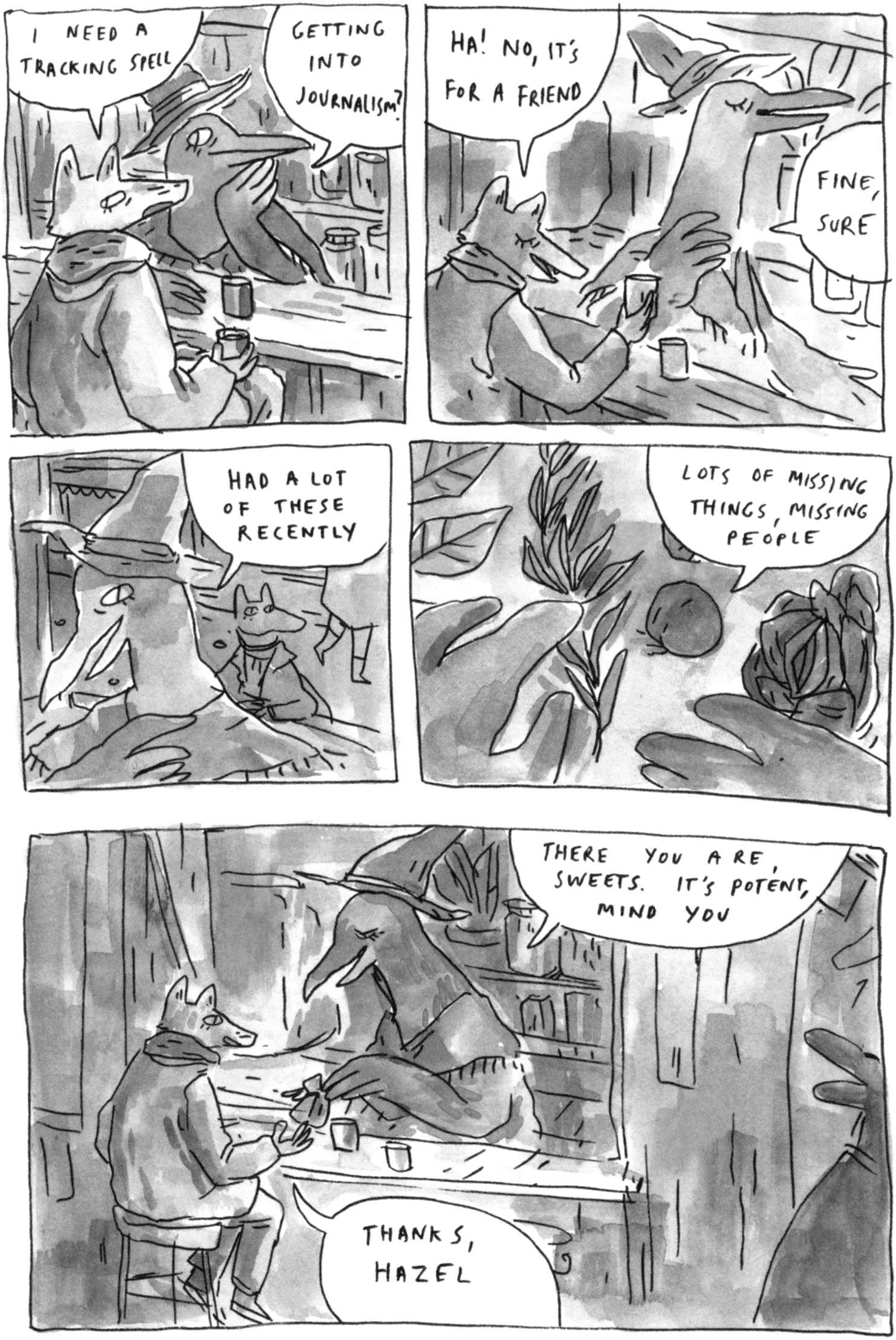
I NEED A TRACKING SPELL
GETTING INTO JOURNALISM?
HA! NO, IT'S FOR A FRIEND
FINE, SURE
HAD A LOT OF THESE RECENTLY
LOTS OF MISSING THINGS, MISSING PEOPLE
THERE YOU ARE, SWEETS. IT'S POTENT, MIND YOU
THANKS, HAZEL

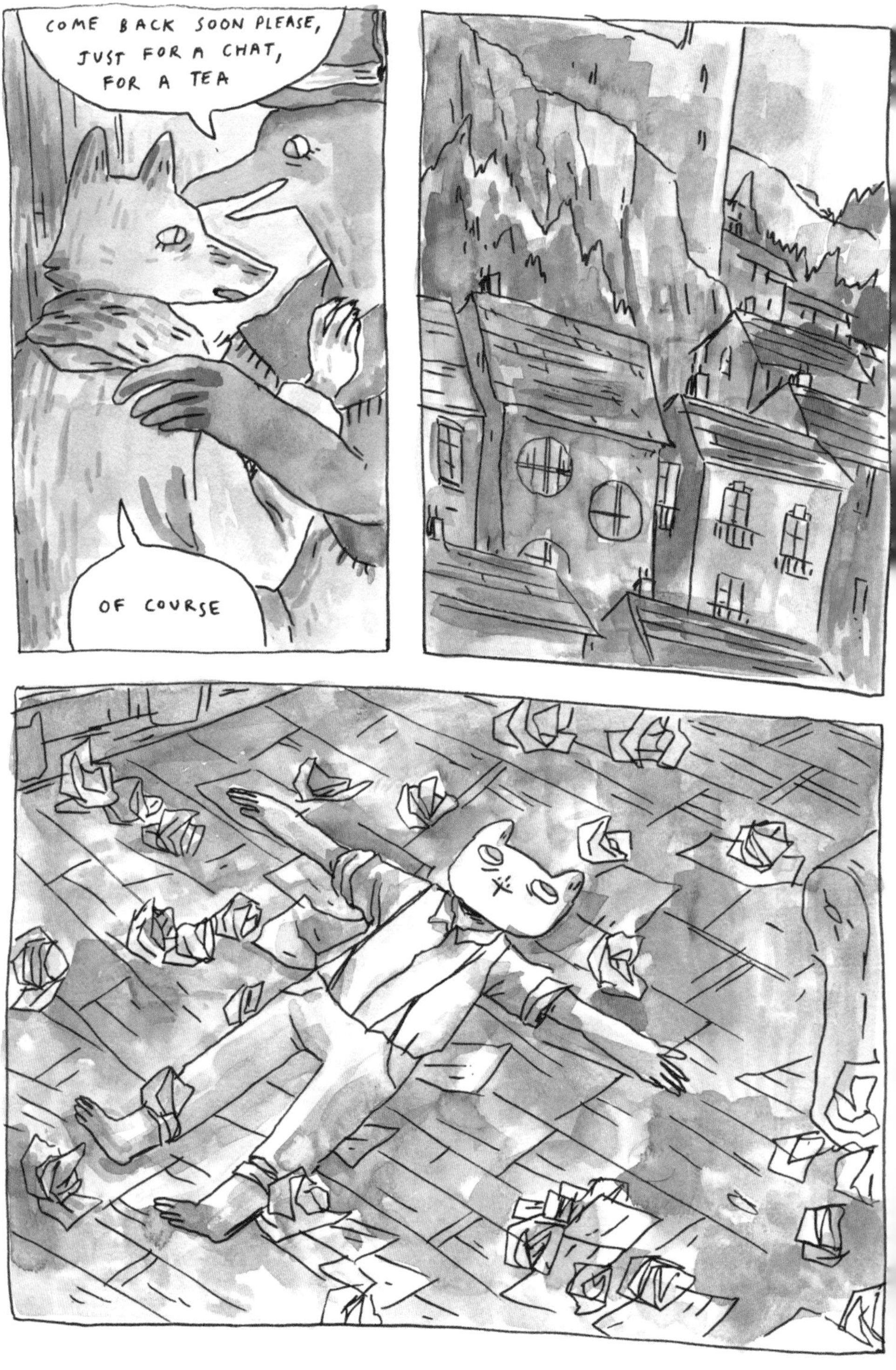
COME BACK SOON PLEASE, JUST FOR A CHAT, FOR A TEA
OF COURSE

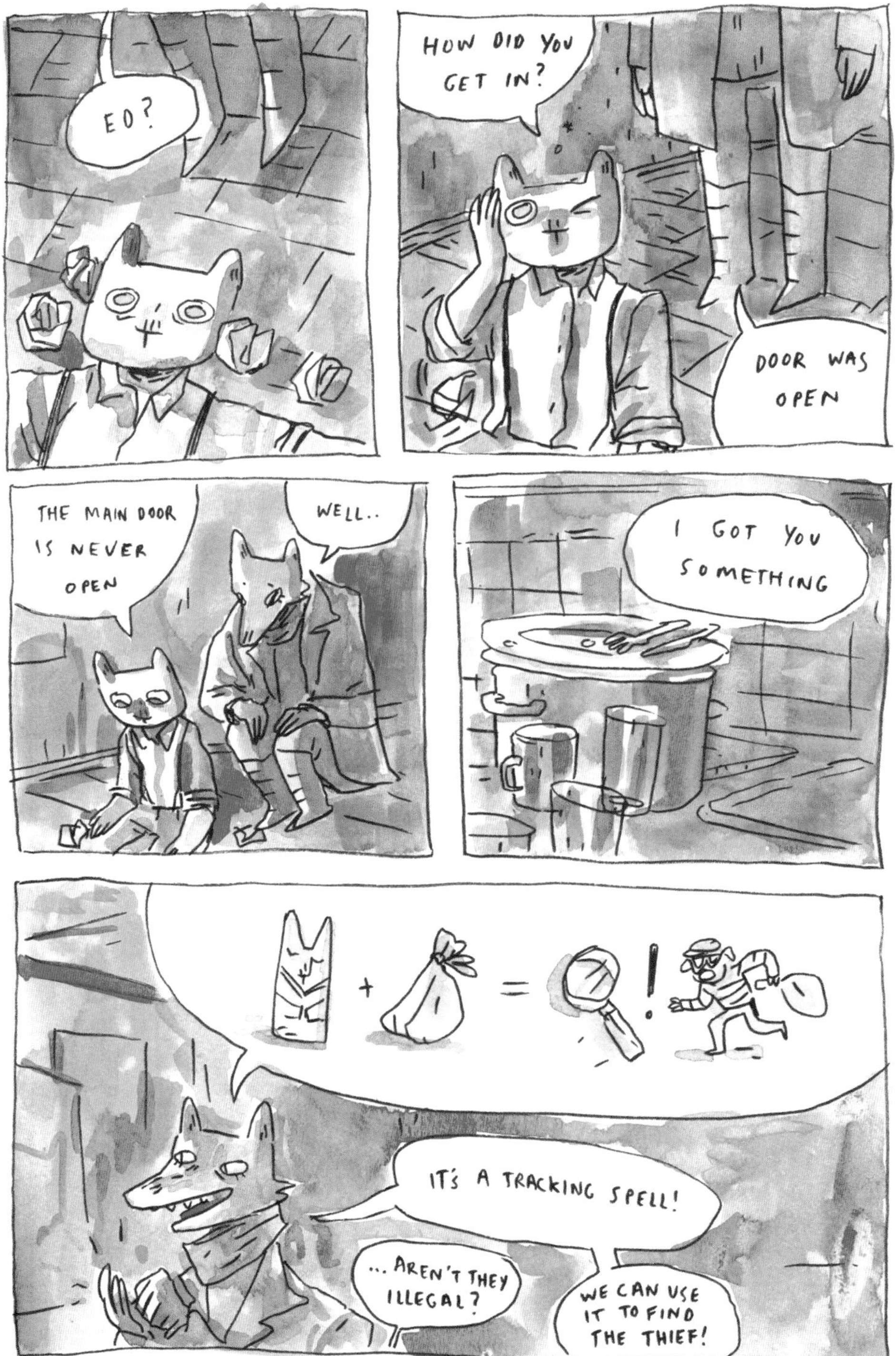
ED?
HOW DID YOU GET IN?
DOOR WAS OPEN
THE MAIN DOOR IS NEVER OPEN
WELL..
I GOT YOU SOMETHING
+
=
!
IT'S A TRACKING SPELL!
WE CAN USE IT TO FIND THE THIEF!
... AREN'T THEY ILLEGAL?

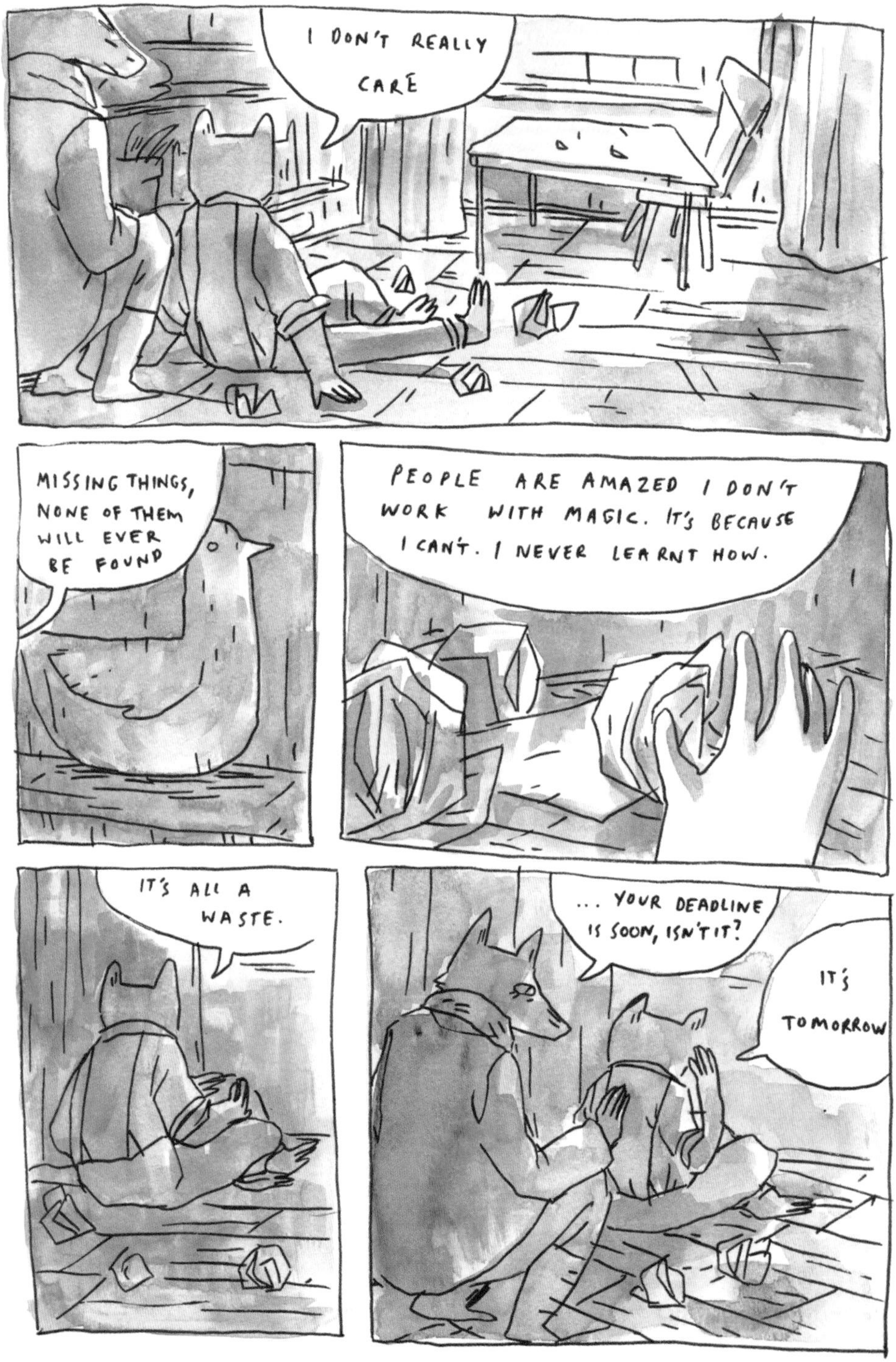
I DON'T REALLY CARE
MISSING THINGS, NONE OF THEM WILL EVER BE FOUND
PEOPLE ARE AMAZED I DON'T WORK WITH MAGIC. IT'S BECAUSE I CAN'T. I NEVER LEARNT HOW.
IT'S ALL A WASTE.
... YOUR DEADLINE IS SOON, ISN'T IT?
IT'S TOMORROW

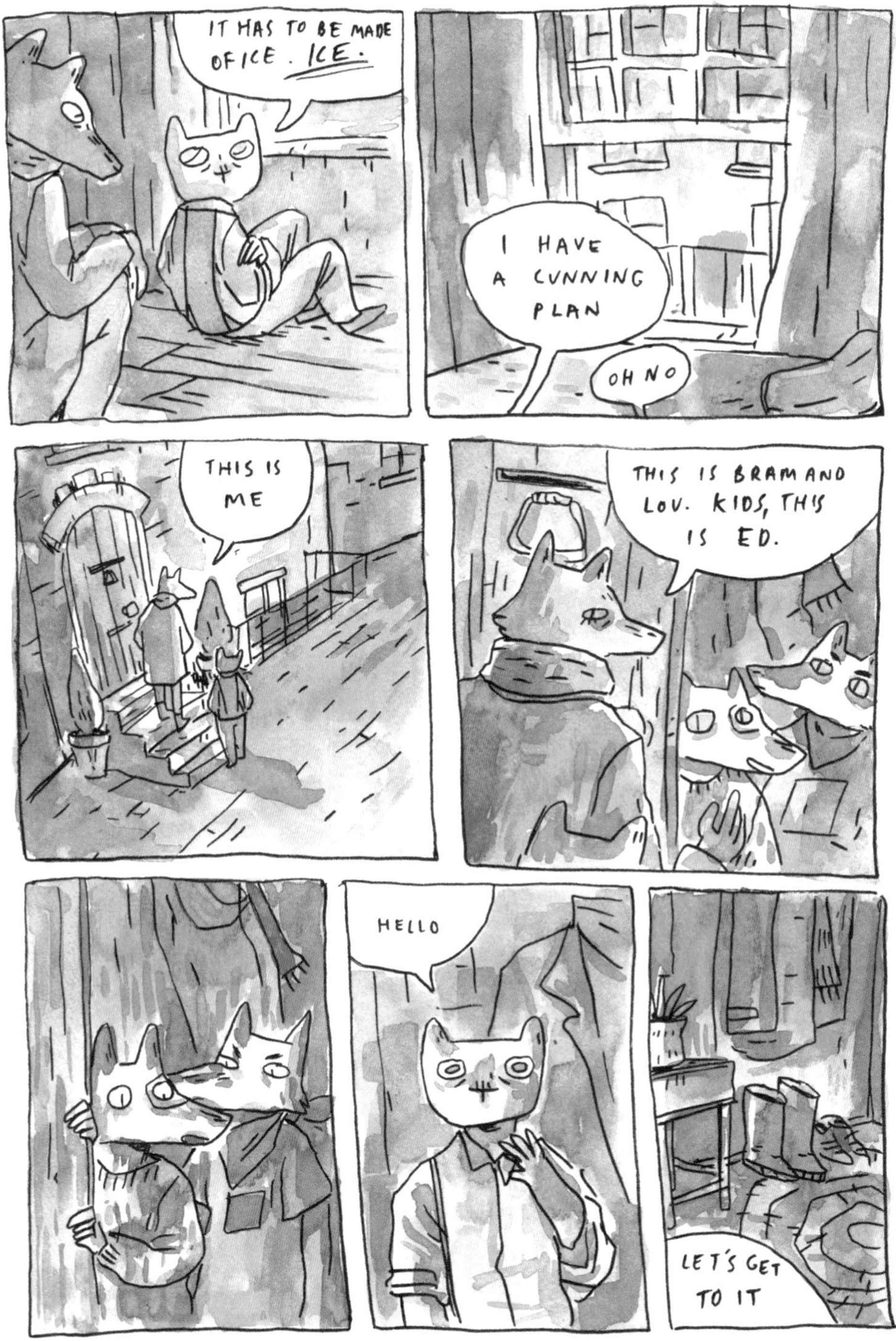
IT HAS TO BE MADE OF ICE. ICE.
I HAVE A CUNNING PLAN
OH NO
THIS IS ME
THIS IS BRAM AND LOV. KIDS, THIS IS ED.
HELLO
LET'S GET TO IT

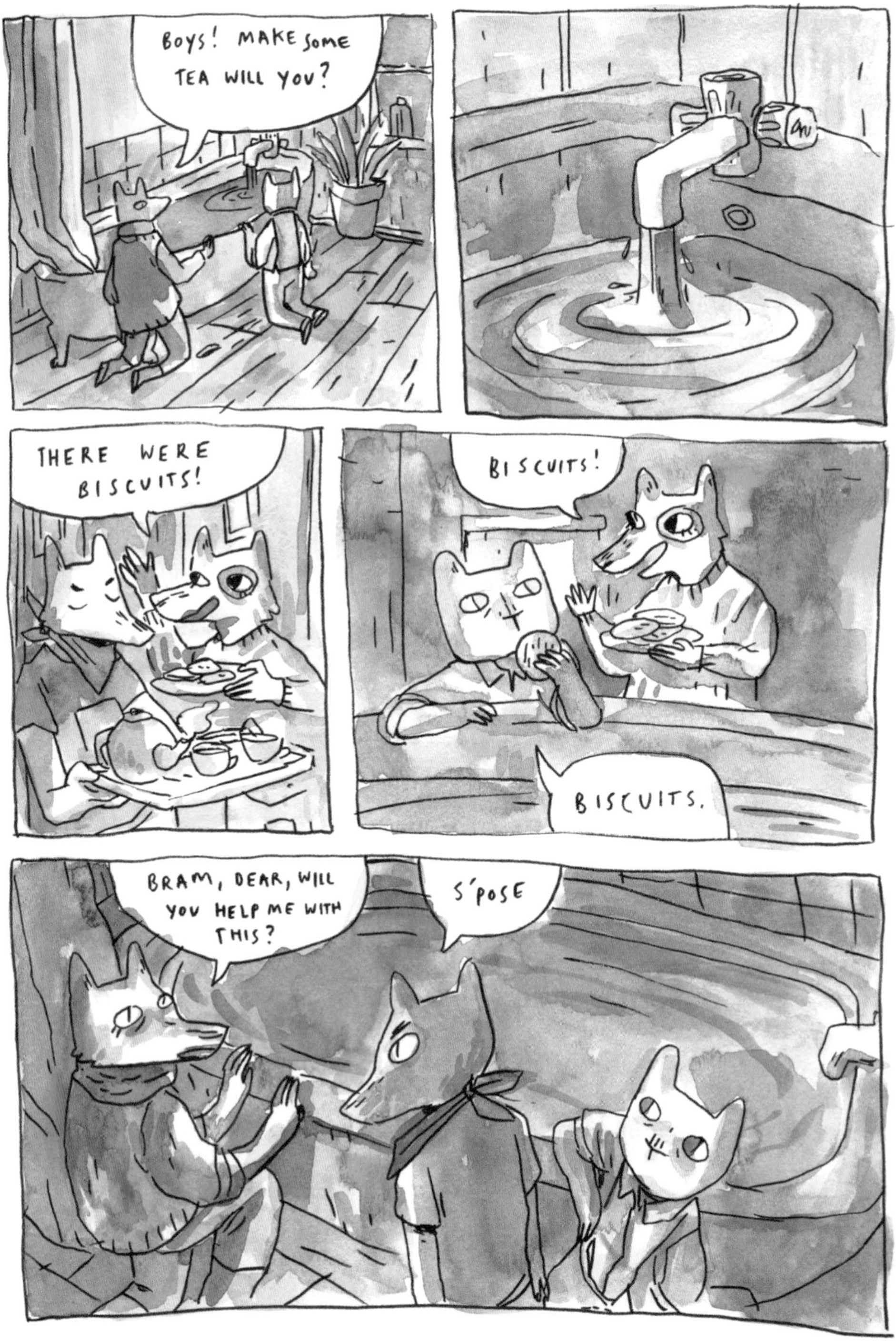
BOYS! MAKE SOME TEA WILL YOU?
THERE WERE BISCUITS!
BISCUITS!
BISCUITS.
BRAM, DEAR, WILL YOU HELP ME WITH THIS?
S'POSE

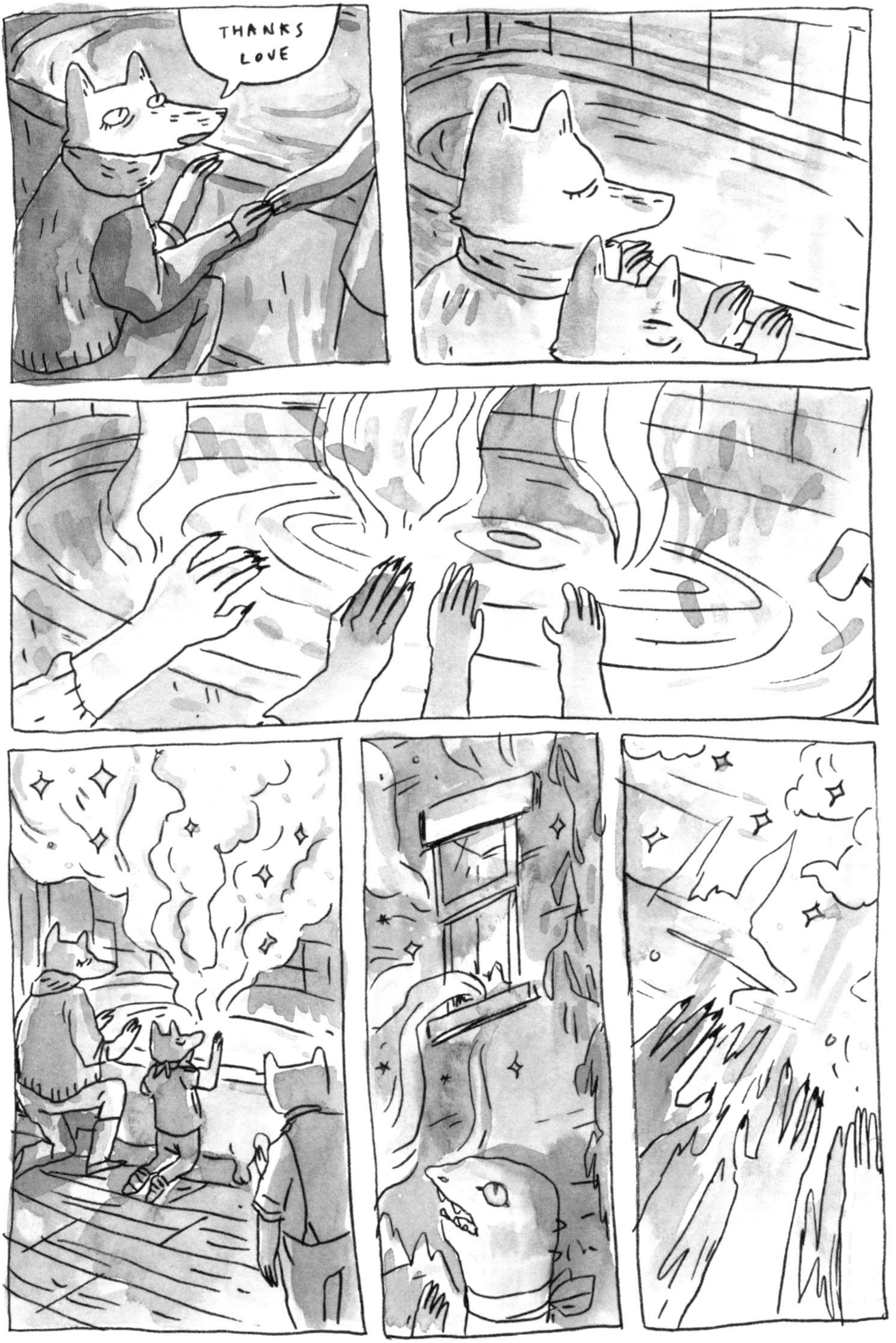
THANKS LOVE

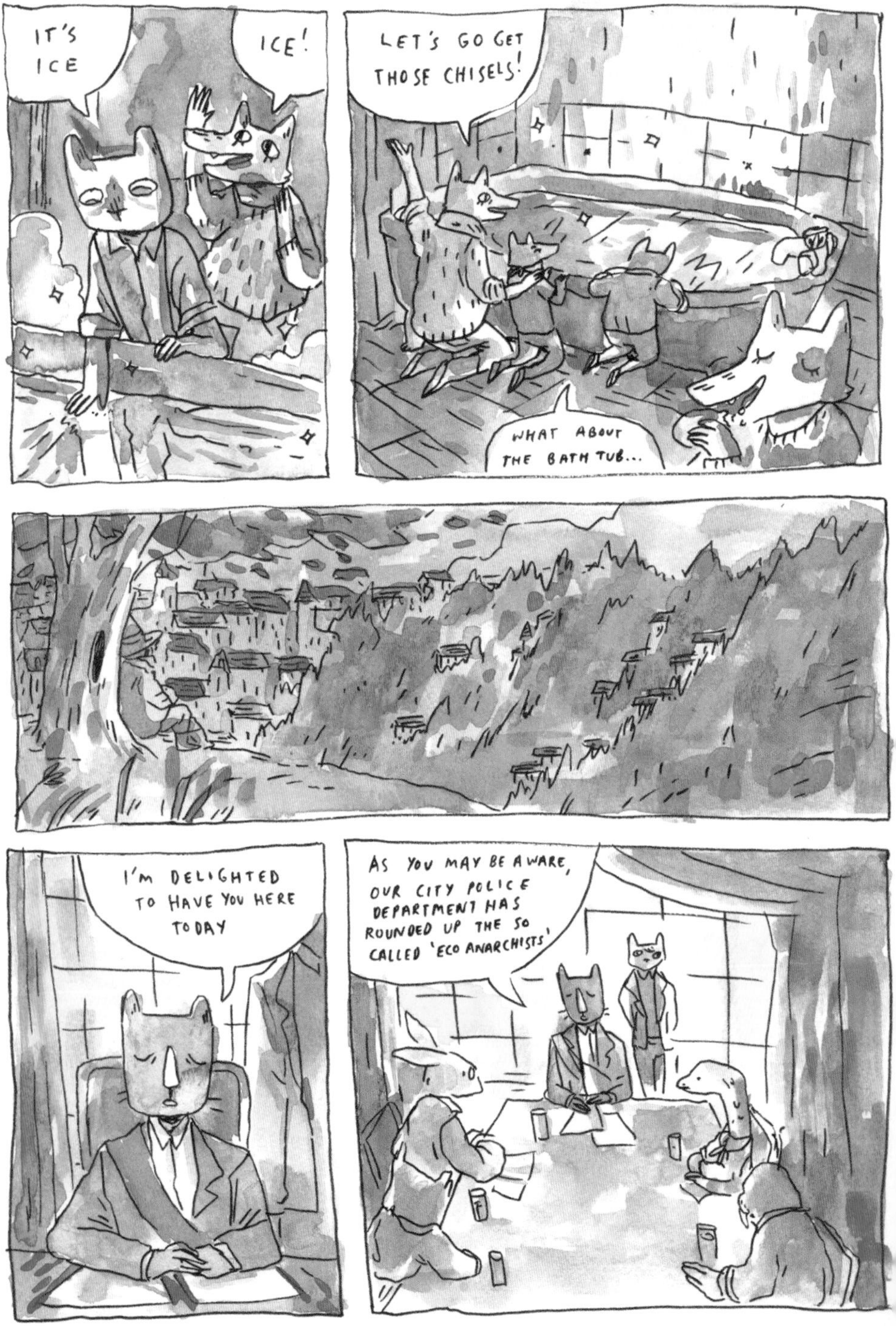
IT'S ICE
ICE!
LET'S GO GET THOSE CHISELS!
WHAT ABOUT THE BATH TUB...
I'M DELIGHTED TO HAVE YOU HERE TODAY
AS YOU MAY BE AWARE, OUR CITY POLICE DEPARTMENT HAS ROUNDED UP THE SO CALLED 'ECO ANARCHISTS'

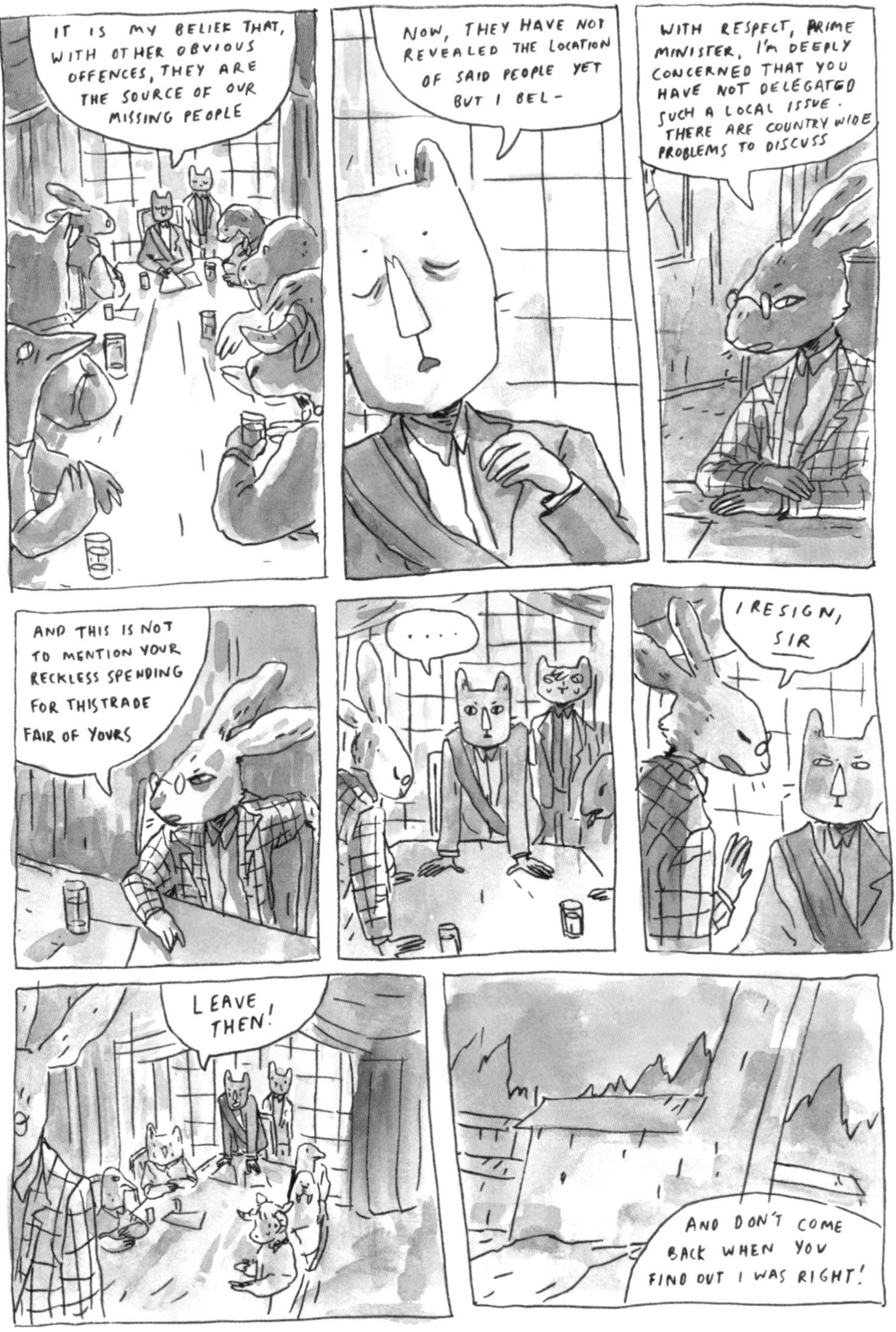
IT IS MY BELIEF THAT, WITH OTHER OBVIOUS OFFENCES, THEY ARE THE SOURCE OF OUR MISSING PEOPLE
NOW, THEY HAVE NOT REVEALED THE LOCATION OF SAID PEOPLE YET BUT I BEL-
WITH RESPECT, PRIME MINISTER, I'M DEEPLY CONCERNED THAT YOU HAVE NOT DELEGATED SUCH A LOCAL ISSUE. THERE ARE COUNTRY WIDE PROBLEMS TO DISCUSS
AND THIS IS NOT TO MENTION YOUR RECKLESS SPENDING FOR THIS TRADE FAIR OF YOURS
. . . .
I RESIGN, SIR
LEAVE THEN!
AND DON'T COME BACK WHEN YOU FIND OUT I WAS RIGHT!

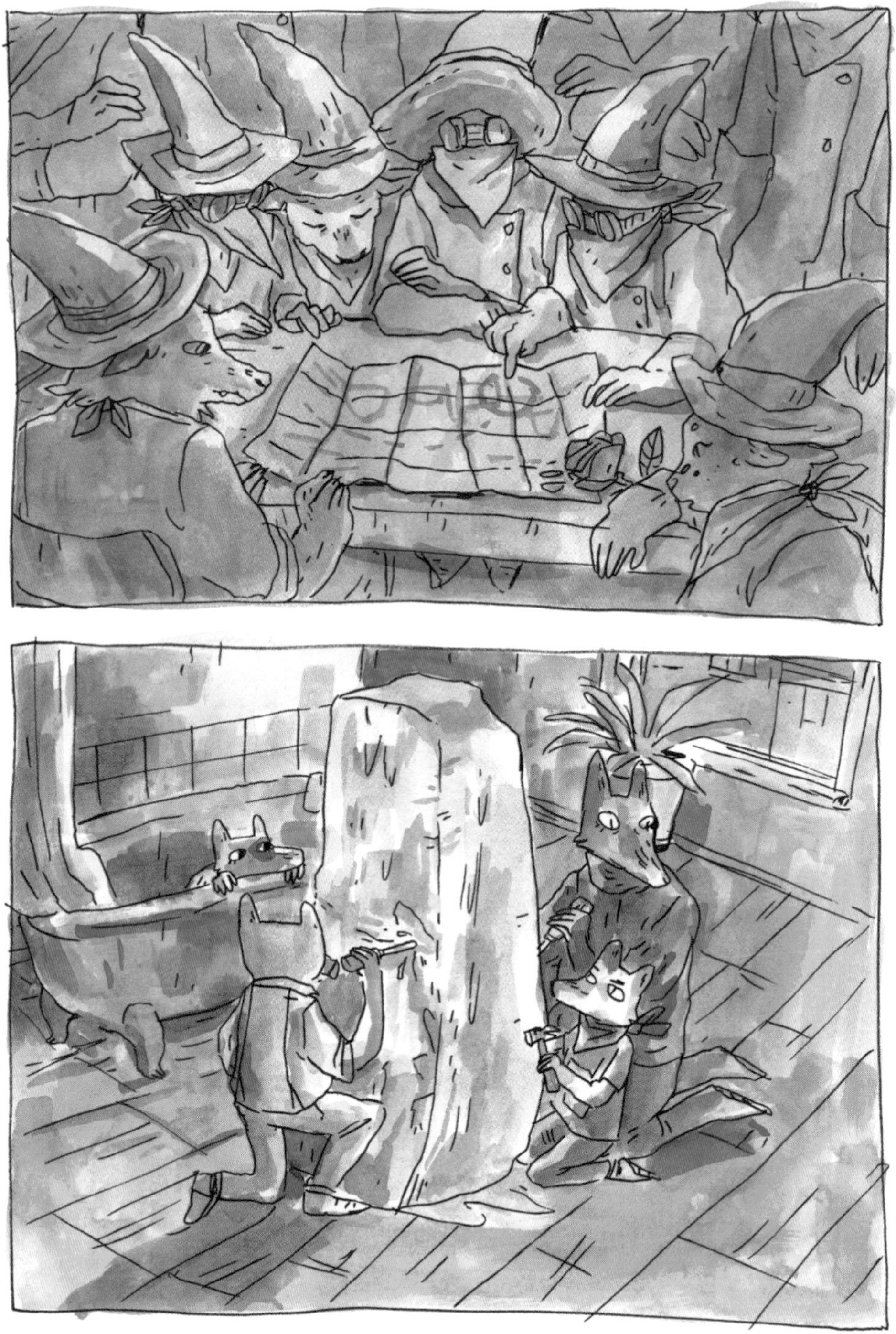

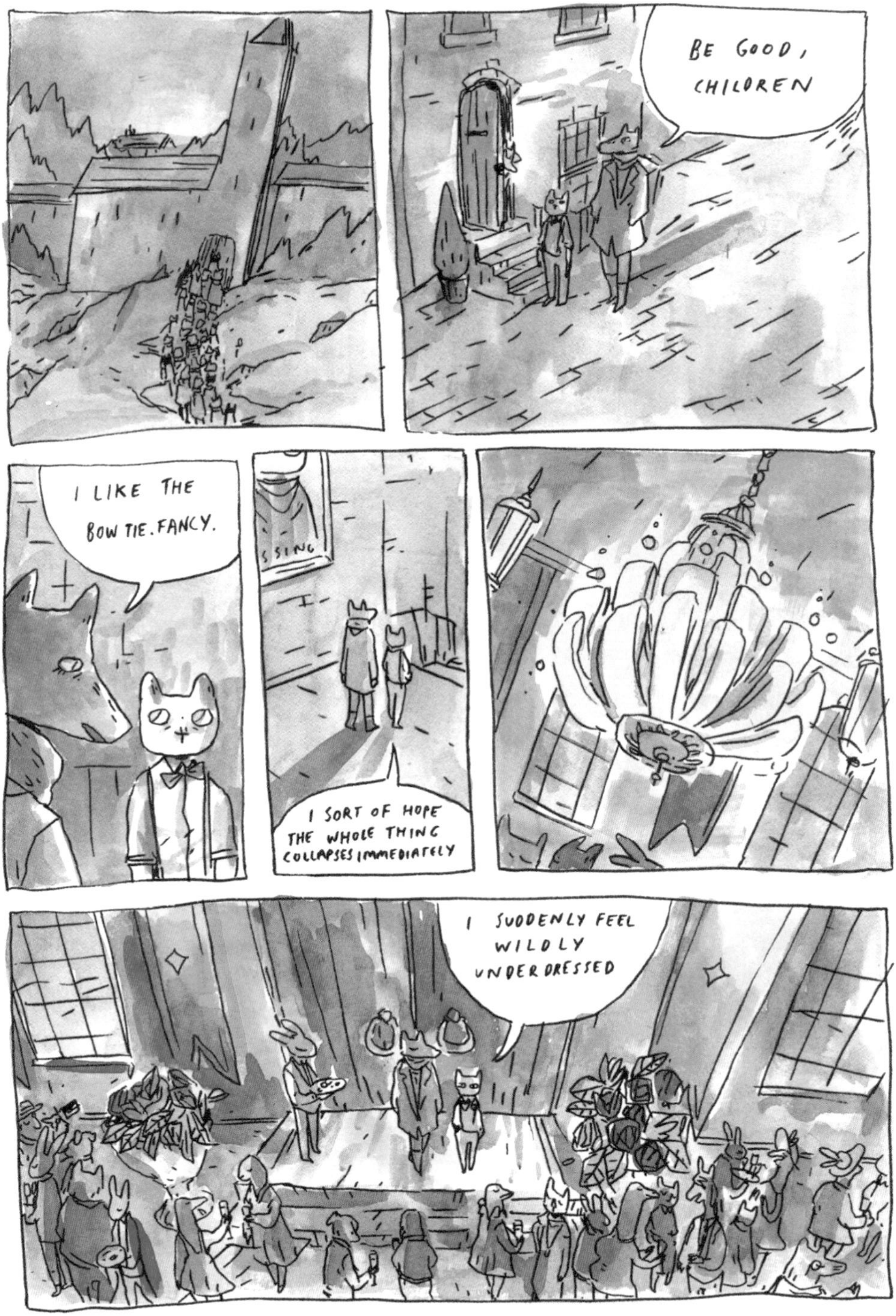
BE GOOD, CHILDREN
I LIKE THE BOW TIE. FANCY.
SSING
I SORT OF HOPE THE WHOLE THING COLLAPSES IMMEDIATELY
I SUDDENLY FEEL WILDLY UNDERDRESSED

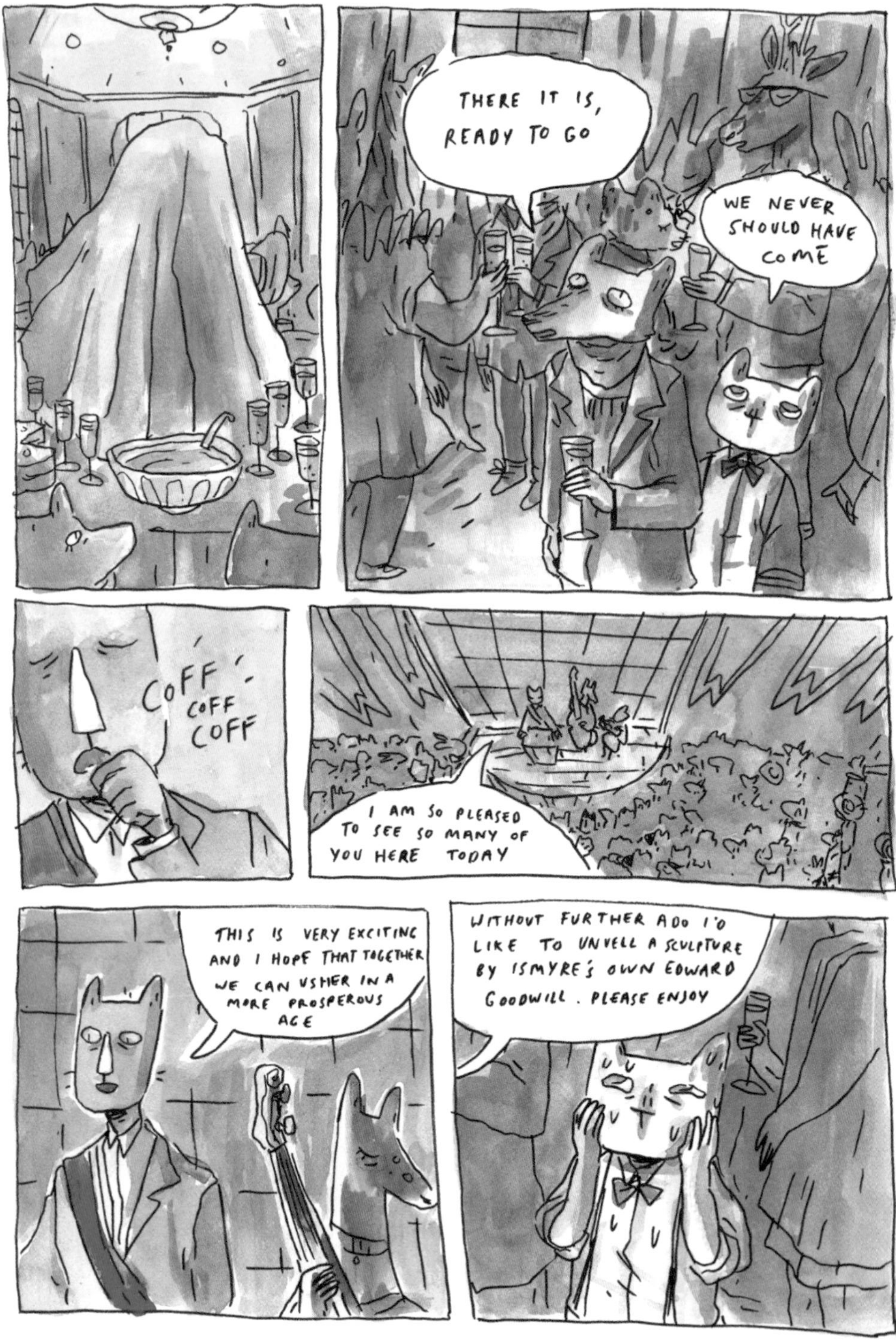
THERE IT IS, READY TO GO
WE NEVER SHOULD HAVE COME
COFF COFF COFF
I AM SO PLEASED TO SEE SO MANY OF YOU HERE TODAY
THIS IS VERY EXCITING AND I HOPE THAT TOGETHER WE CAN USHER IN A MORE PROSPEROUS AGE
WITHOUT FURTHER ADO I'D LIKE TO UNVEIL A SCULPTURE BY ISMYRE'S OWN EDWARD GOODWILL. PLEASE ENJOY

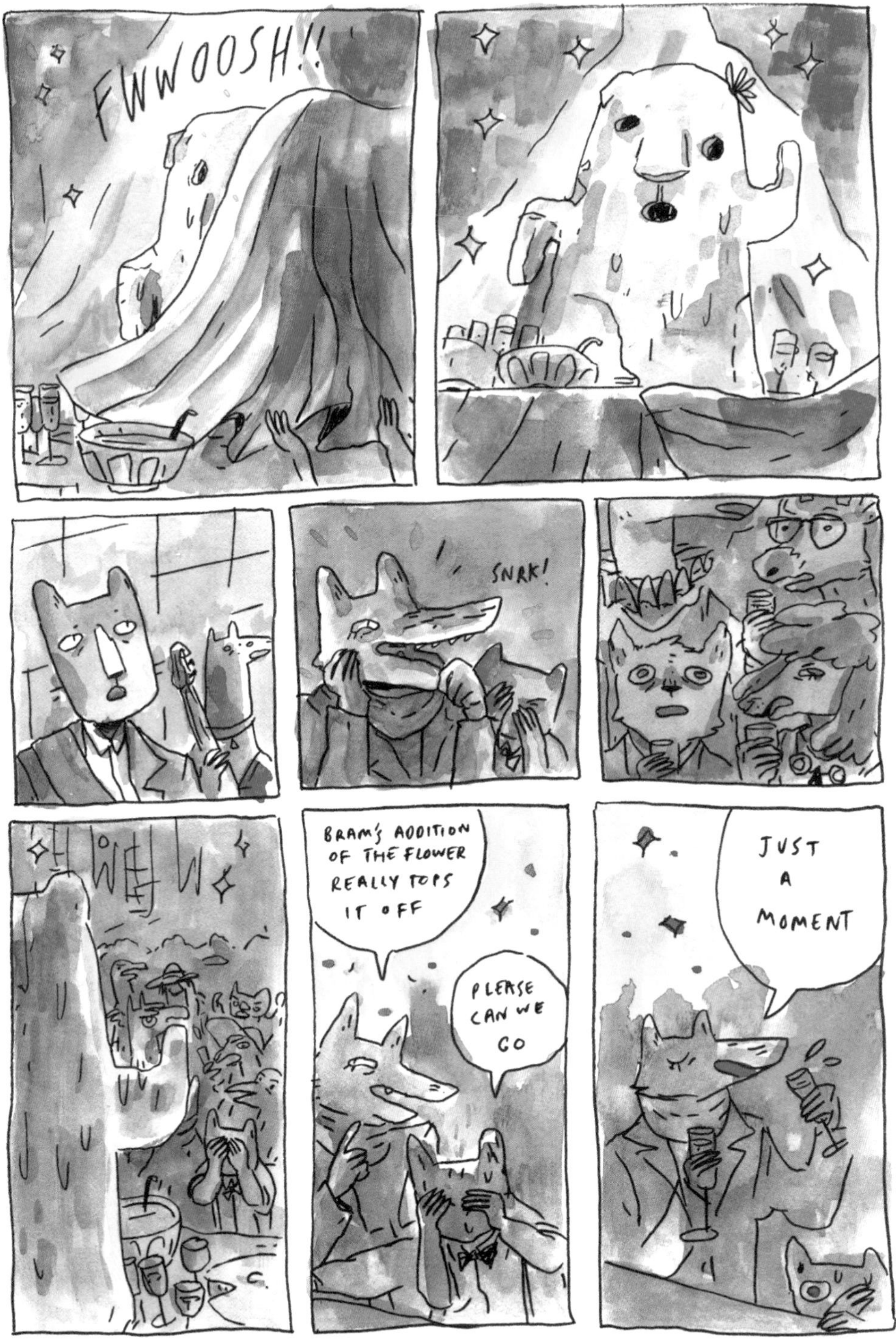
FWWOOSH!!
SNRK!
BRAM'S ADDITION OF THE FLOWER REALLY TOPS IT OFF
PLEASE CAN WE GO
JUST A MOMENT

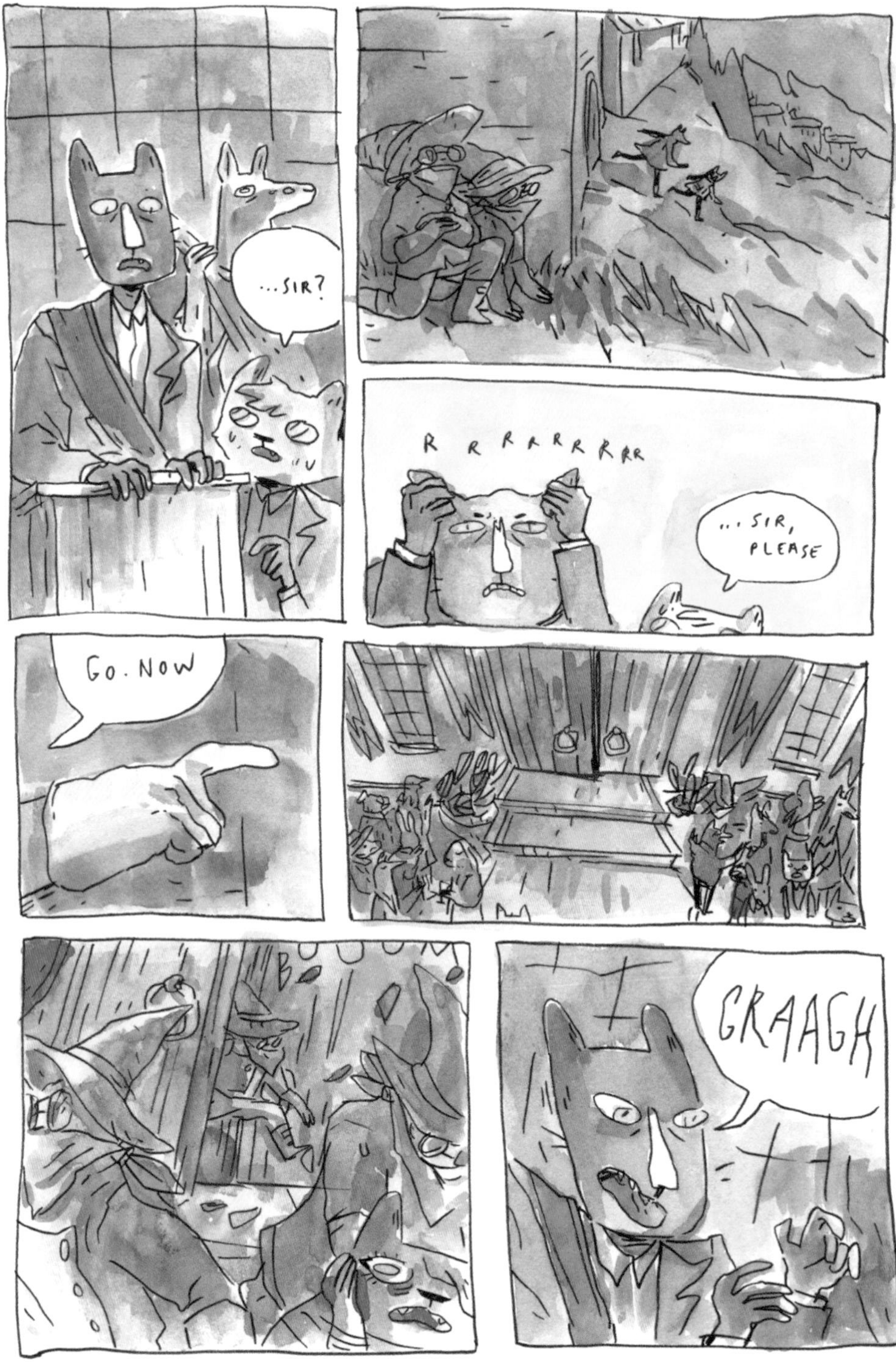
...SIR?
R R RRRRRRRR
...SIR, PLEASE
GO. NOW
GRAAGH

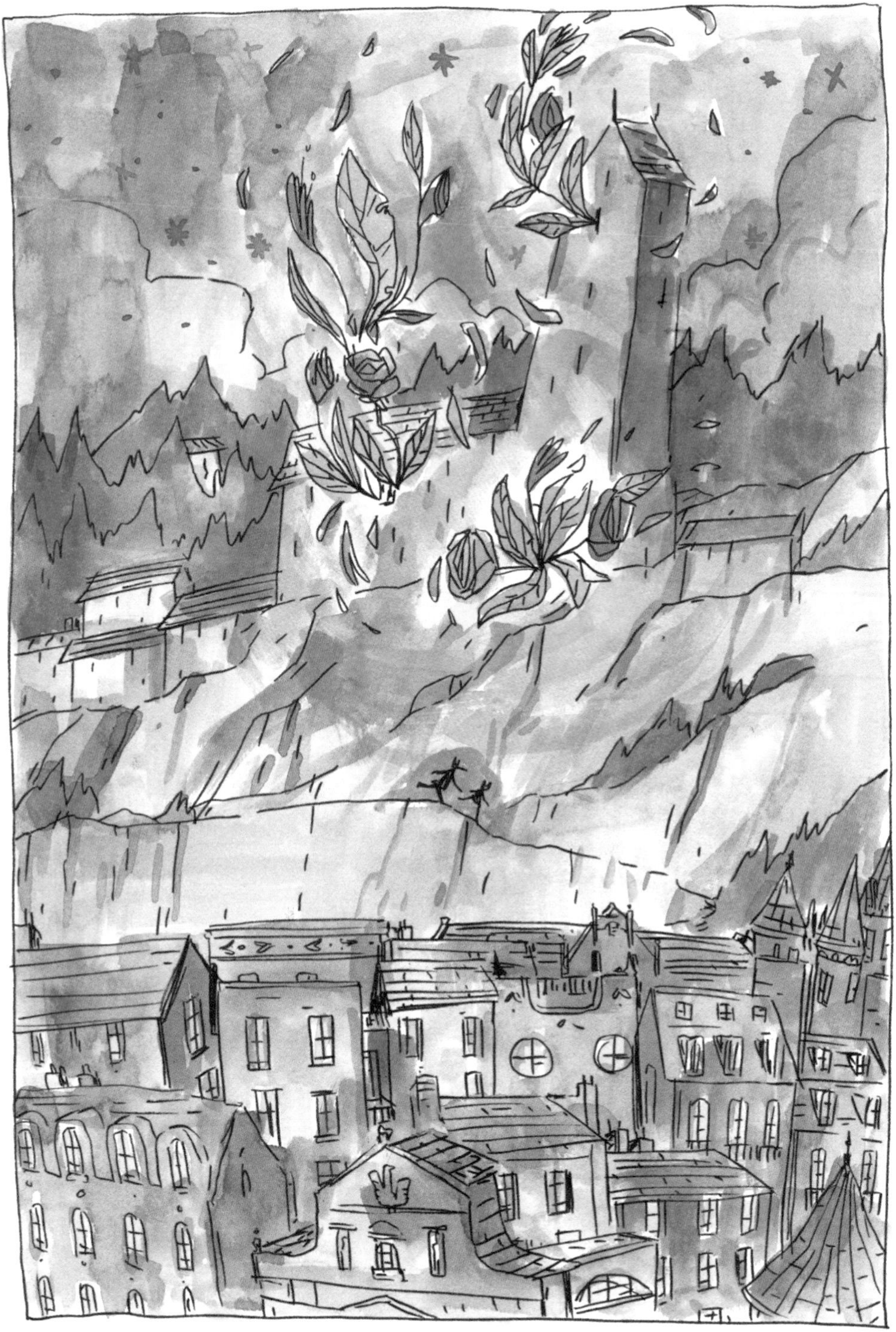

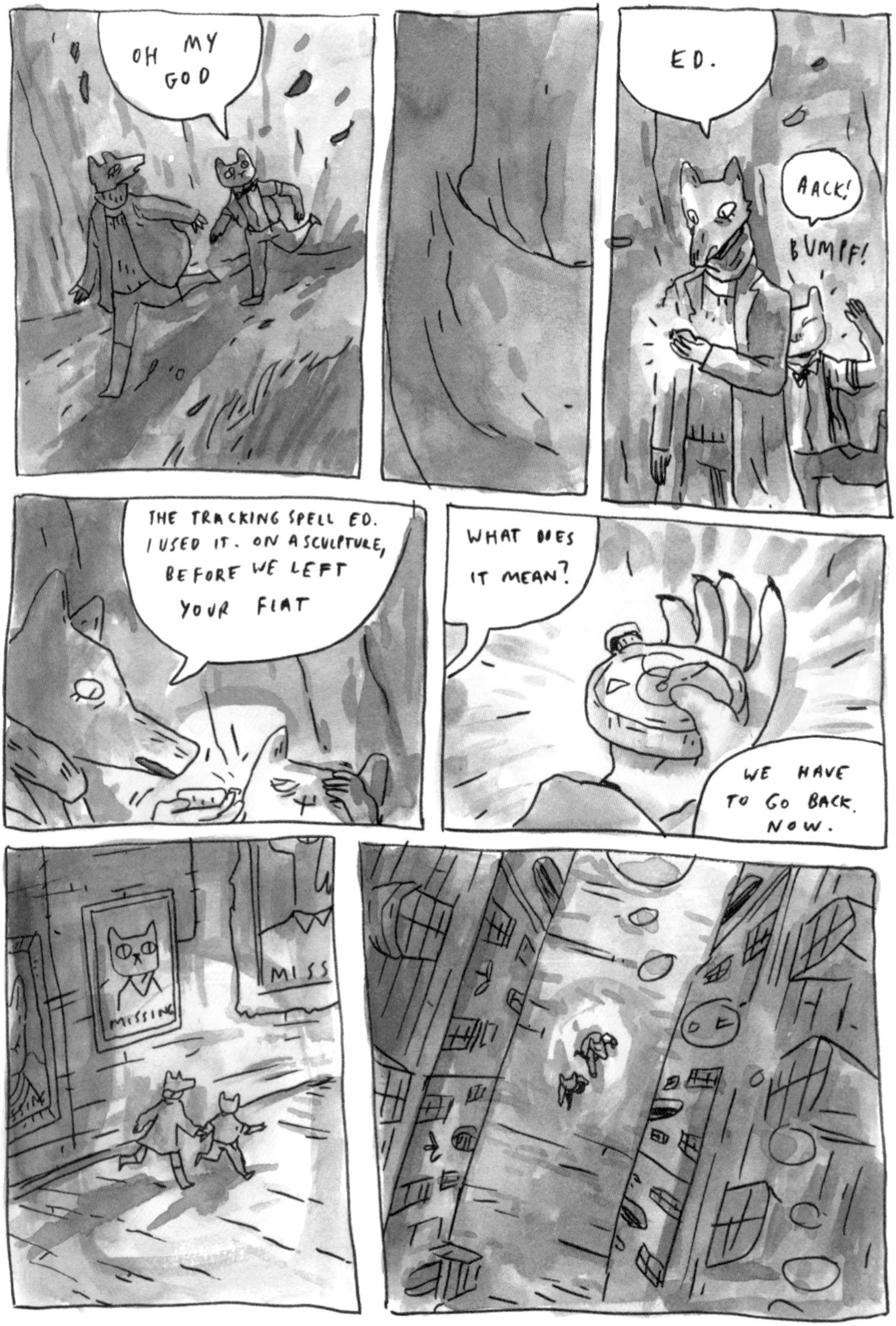
OH MY GOD
ED.
AACK!
BUMPF!
THE TRACKING SPELL ED. I USED IT. ON A SCULPTURE, BEFORE WE LEFT YOUR FLAT
WHAT DOES IT MEAN?
WE HAVE TO GO BACK. NOW.
MISSING
MISS

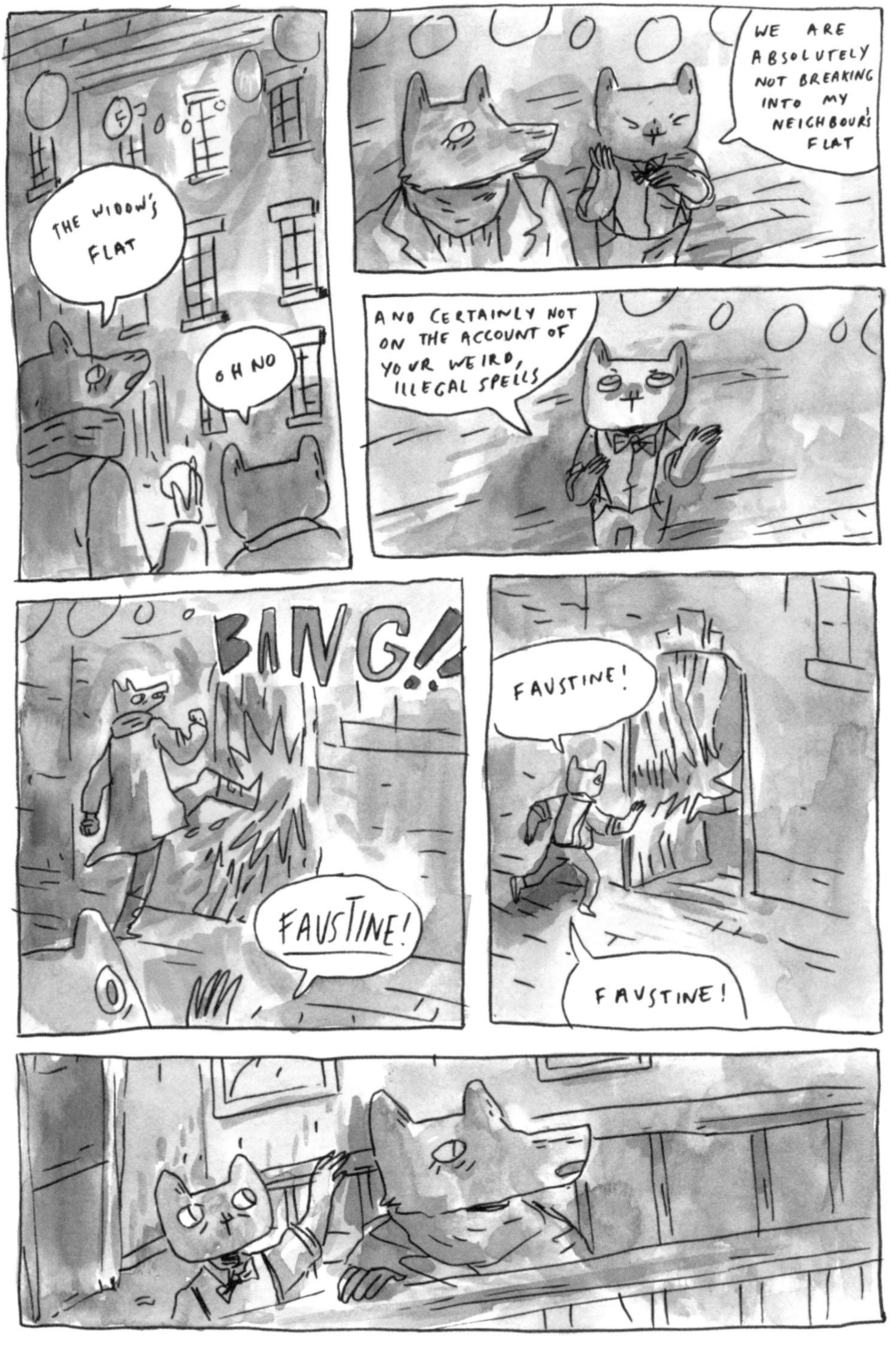
THE WIDOW'S FLAT
OH NO
WE ARE ABSOLUTELY NOT BREAKING INTO MY NEIGHBOUR'S FLAT
AND CERTAINLY NOT ON THE ACCOUNT OF YOUR WEIRD, ILLEGAL SPELLS
BANG!!
FAUSTINE!
FAUSTINE!
FAUSTINE!

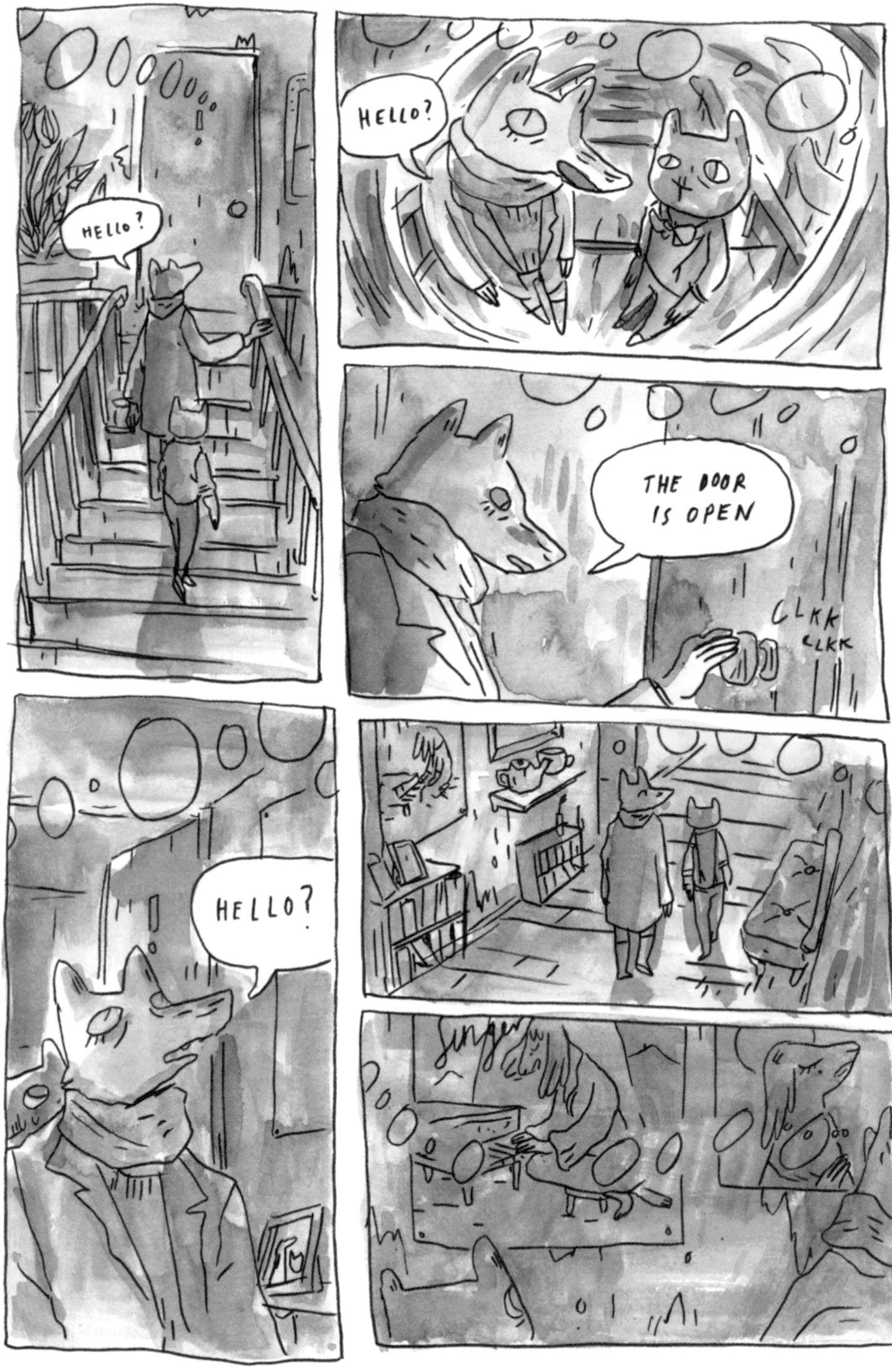
HELLO?
HELLO?
THE DOOR IS OPEN
CLKK CLKK
HELLO?
Singer

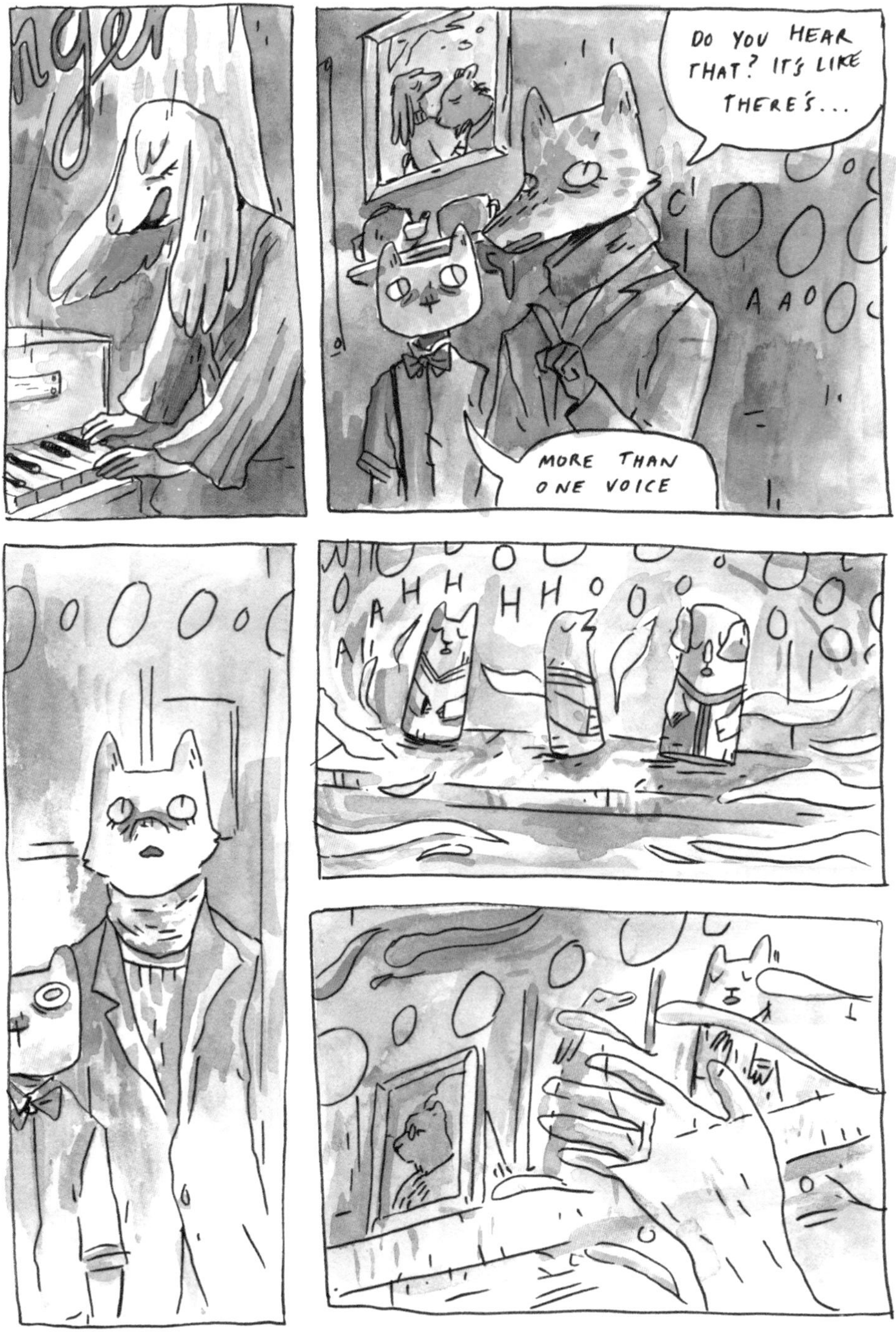
ngel
DO YOU HEAR THAT? IT'S LIKE THERE'S...
OOO
AAO
MORE THAN ONE VOICE
OOOOO
AAHH HHOOO

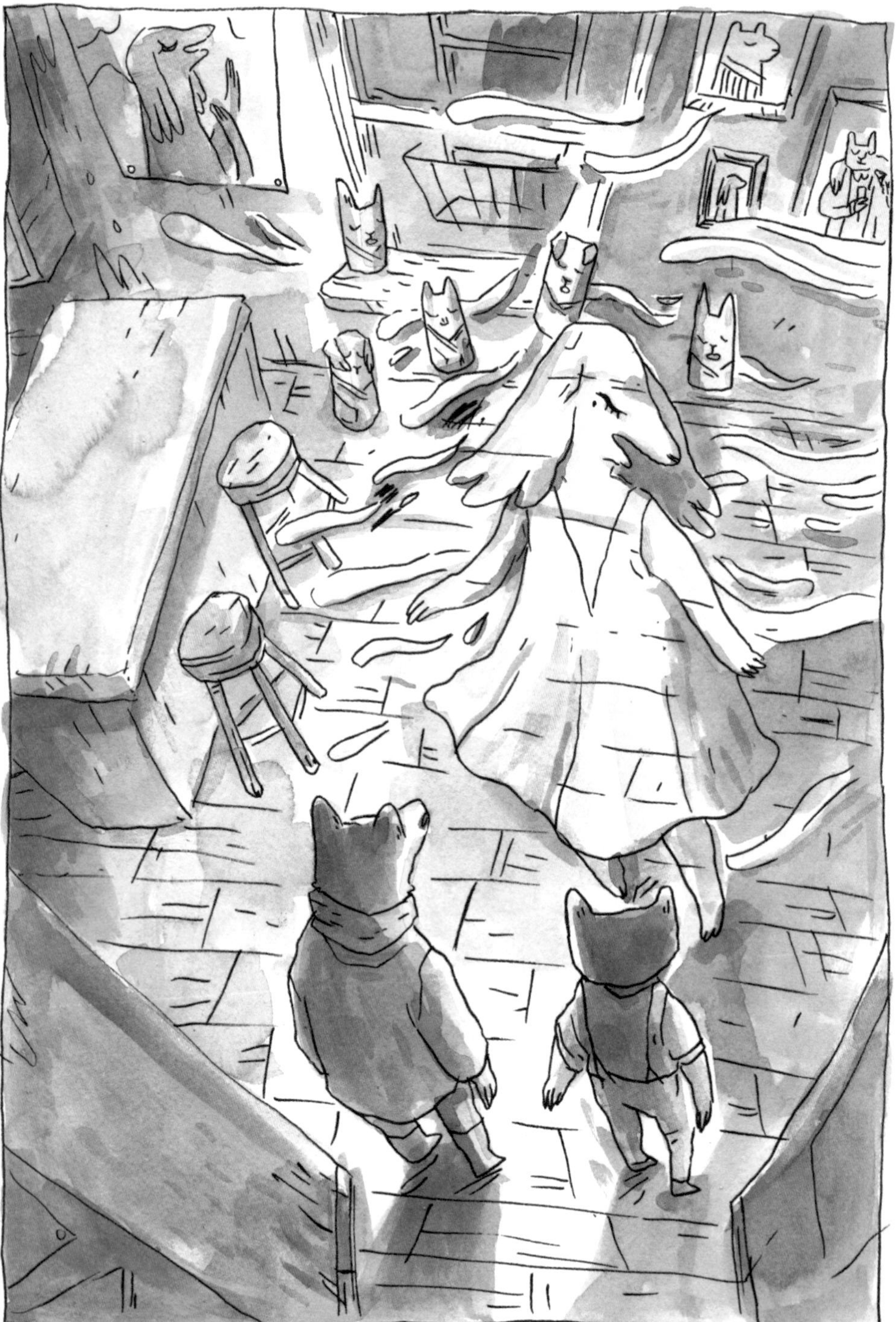

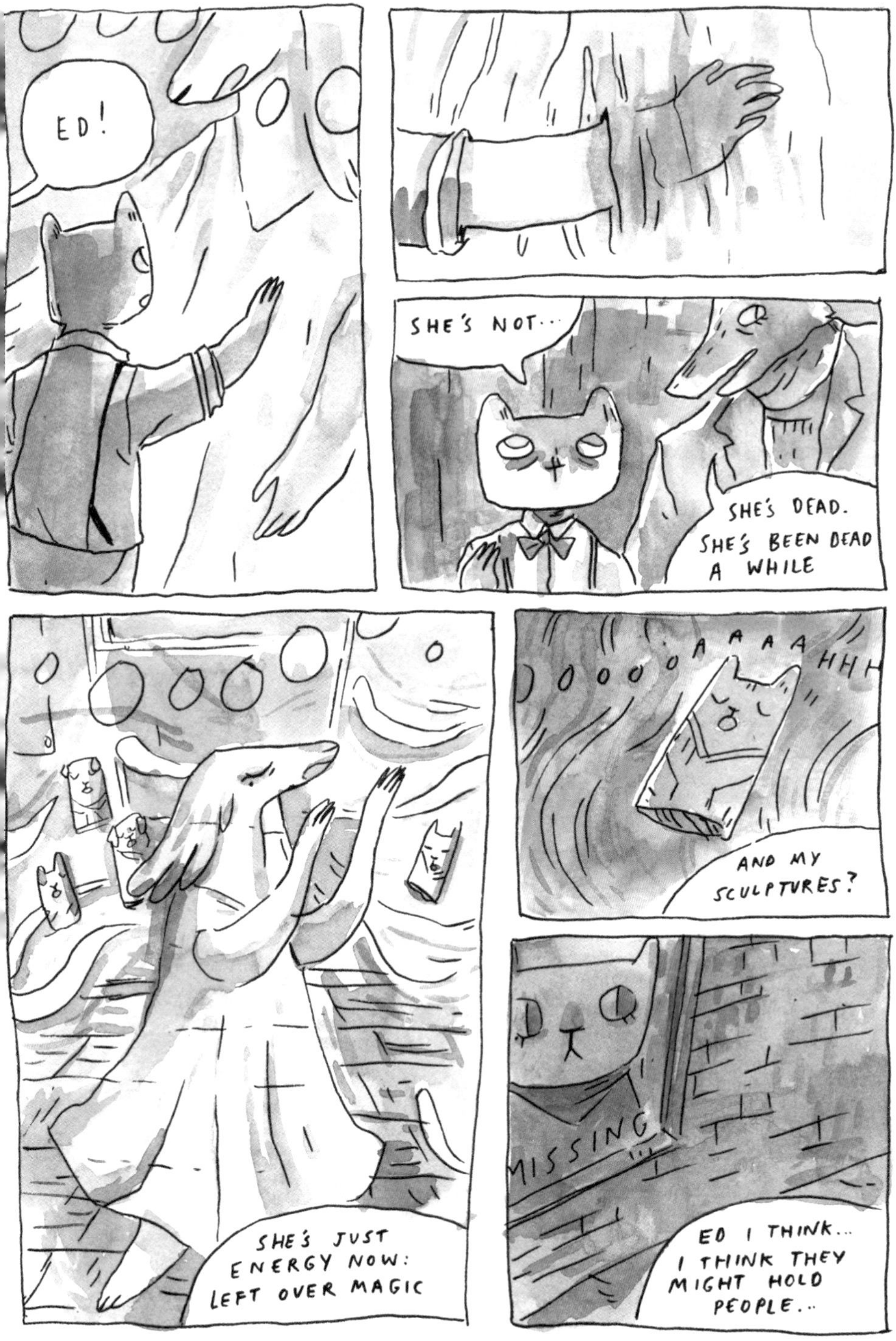
ED!
SHE'S NOT...
SHE'S DEAD. SHE'S BEEN DEAD A WHILE
SHE'S JUST ENERGY NOW: LEFT OVER MAGIC
OOOOOAAAAAHHH
AND MY SCULPTURES?
MISSING
ED I THINK... I THINK THEY MIGHT HOLD PEOPLE...

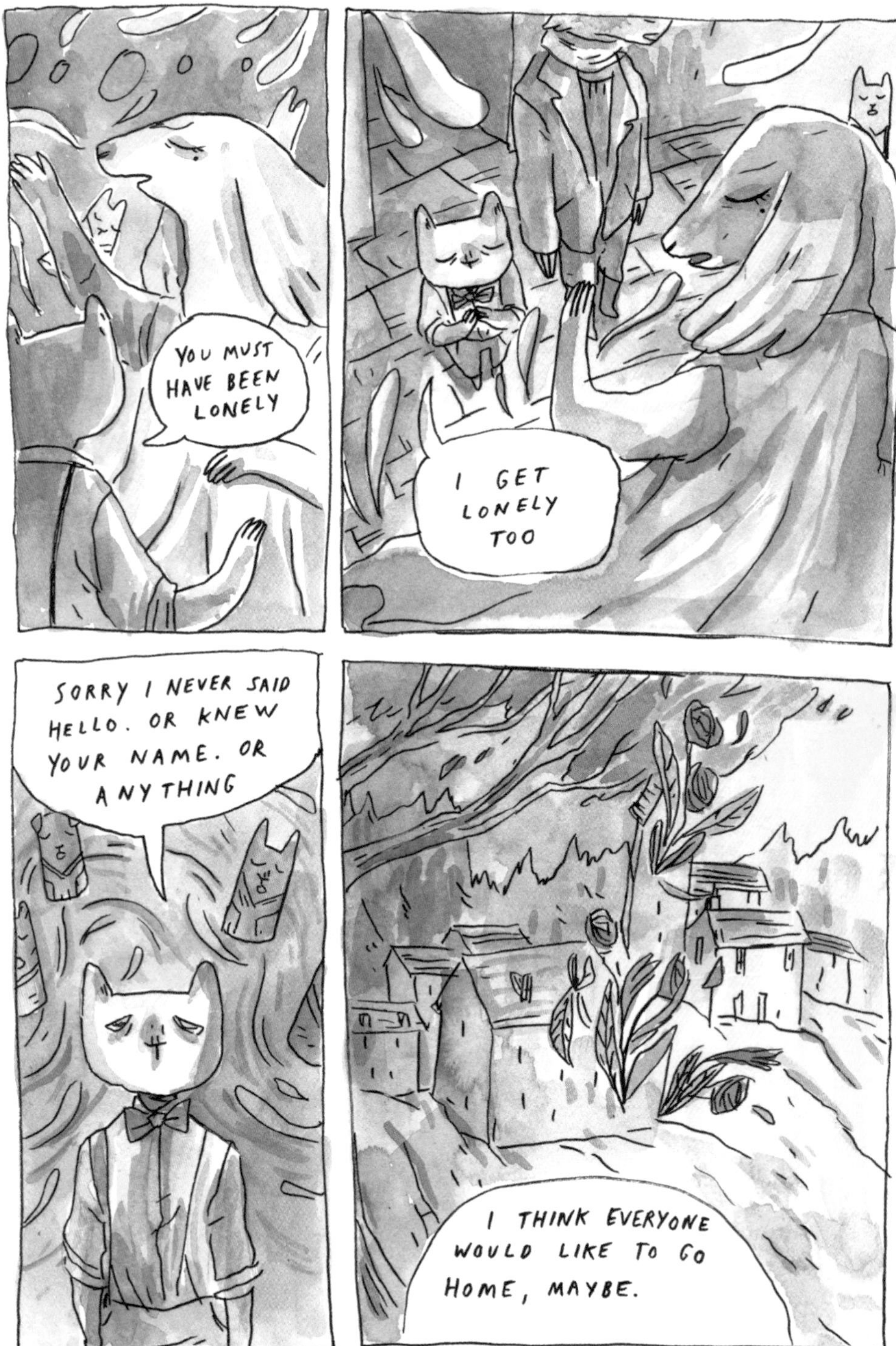
YOU MUST HAVE BEEN LONELY
I GET LONELY TOO
SORRY I NEVER SAID HELLO. OR KNEW YOUR NAME. OR ANYTHING
I THINK EVERYONE WOULD LIKE TO GO HOME, MAYBE.

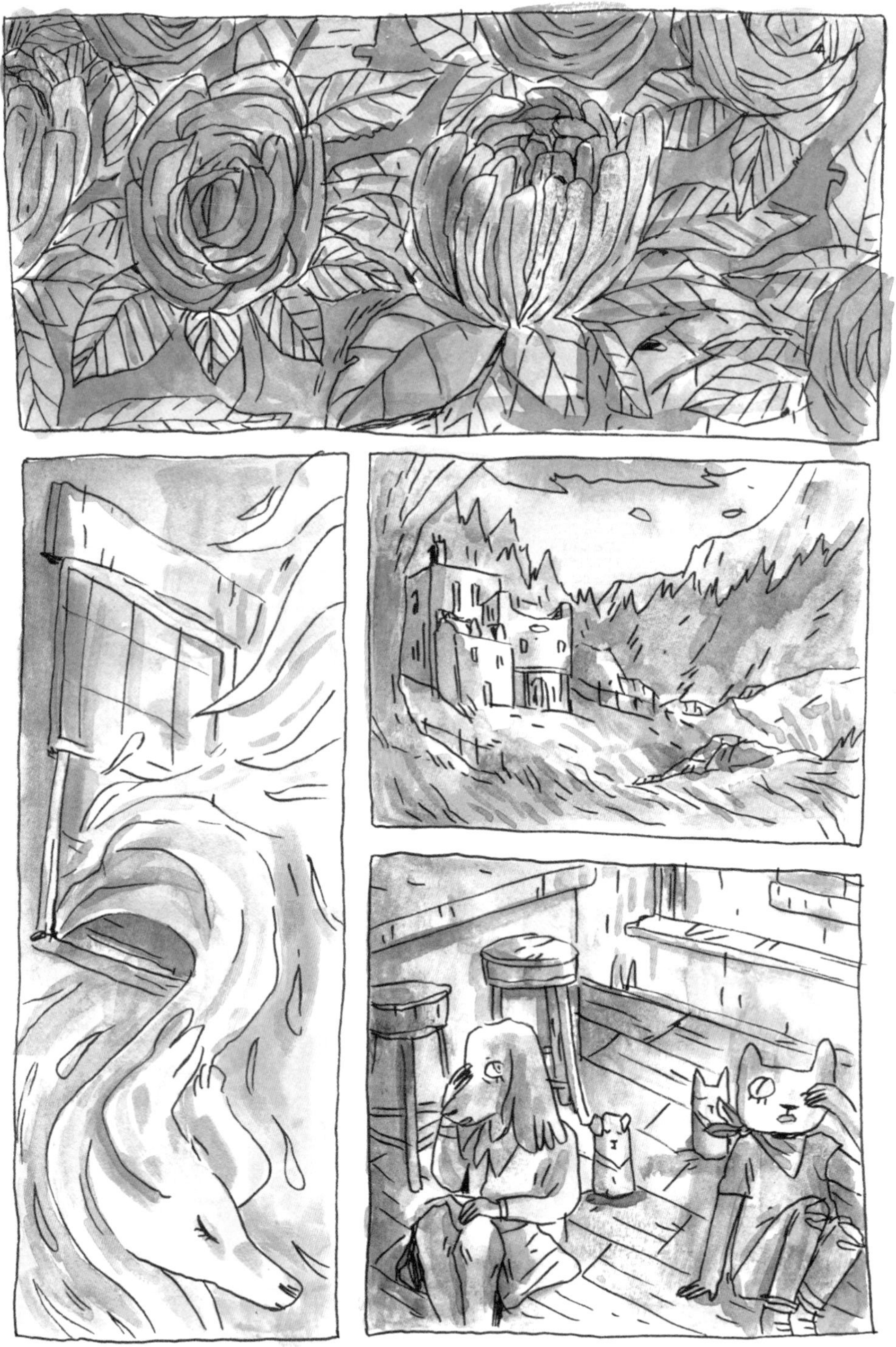

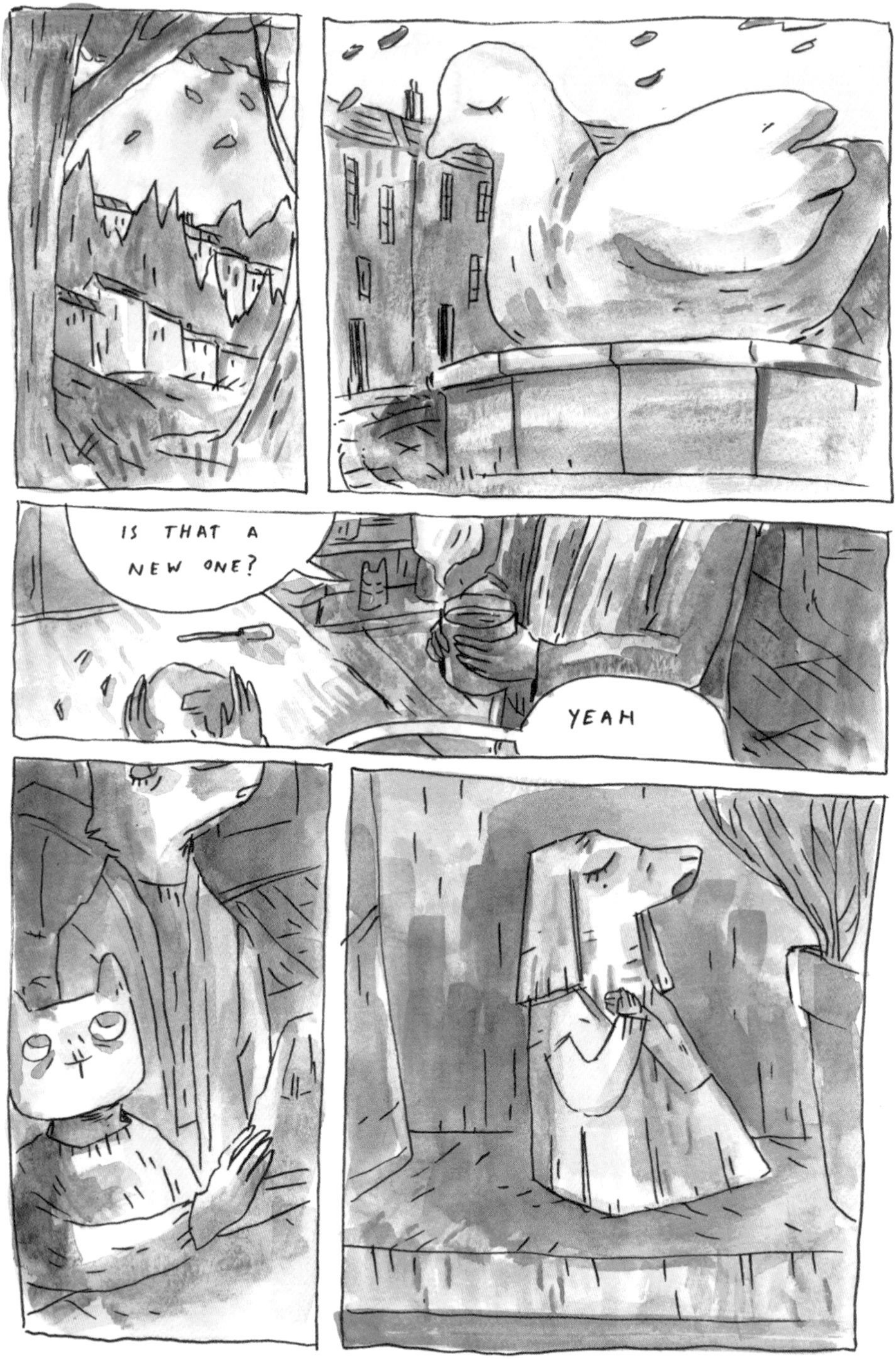
IS THAT A NEW ONE?
YEAH

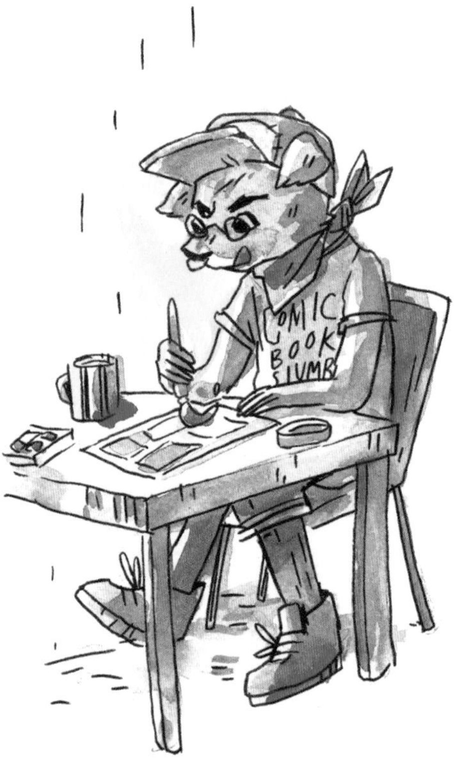
COMIC BOOK SLUMB

THANKYOU TO EVERYONE WHO HELPED AND SUPPORTED ISMYRE! THANKS IF YOU BOUGHT IT AND SPECIAL THANKS TO RICKY, DAVID AND EVERYONE AT AVERY HILL, MY GOOD PAL CHRIS NEAL (AKA ACID LAKE) FOR DOING THE END PAPERS AND MY DOG, FOR MAKING SURE I HAD TO LEAVE THE HOUSE.

I HOPE YOU HAVE ENJOYED THIS WEIRD TALE. I CAN'T WAIT FOR THE NEXT ONE.